COUNTING BACKWARDS

Helen Dunmore (1952-2017) was a poet, novelist, short story and children's writer. Her poetry books received a Poetry Book Society Choice and Recommendations, the Alice Hunt Bartlett Award, and the Signal Poetry Award. *Bestiary* was shortlisted for the T.S. Eliot Prize in 1997. She won first prize in the Cardiff International Poetry Competition in 1990 with her poem 'Sisters leaving the dance', and first prize in the National Poetry Competition in 2010 with 'The Malarkey'.

After making her debut with *The Apple Fall* in 1983, Helen Dunmore published all her poetry with Bloodaxe Books, completing her tenth and final collection, *Inside the Wave*, shortly before her death in 2017. *Inside the Wave* won the 2017 Costa Poetry Award, and went on to be named as Costa Book of the Year, only the second posthumous award in the history of the Costa/Whitbread Book of the Year. *Counting Backwards: Poems 1975-2017*, a retrospective edition drawing on all her collections, was published by Bloodaxe in 2019.

She published twelve novels and three books of short stories with Penguin, including *A Spell of Winter* (1995), winner of the Orange Prize for Fiction, *Talking to the Dead* (1996), *The Siege* (2001), *Mourning Ruby* (2003), *House of Orphans* (2006) and *The Betrayal* (2010), as well as *The Greatcoat* (2012) with Hammer, and *The Lie* (2014) *Exposure* (2016) and *Birdcage Walk* (2017) with Hutchinson. A final short story collection, *Girl, Balancing*, was published by Hutchinson in 2018.

Born in Beverley, Yorkshire, she studied English at York University, and after graduating in 1973 spent two years teaching in Finland before settling in Bristol.

HELEN DUNMORE

COUNTING BACKWARDS

POEMS 1975-2017

BLOODAXE BOOKS

ISBN: 978 1 78037 445 1

First published 2019 by
Bloodaxe Books Ltd,
Eastburn,
South Park,
Hexham,
Northumberland NE46 1BS.

www.bloodaxebooks.com
For further information about Bloodaxe titles
please visit our website and join our mailing list
or write to the above address for a catalogue.

Supported using public funding by
**ARTS COUNCIL
ENGLAND**

Cover design: Neil Astley & Pamela Robertson-Pearce.

Printed in Great Britain by Bell & Bain Limited, Glasgow, Scotland, on
acid-free paper sourced from mills with FSC chain of custody certification.

ACKNOWLEDGEMENTS

This edition of Helen Dunmore's poetry has been expanded from *Out of the Blue: Poems 1975-2001* (Bloodaxe Books, 2001) to include all the poems from her three later Bloodaxe collections *Inside the Wave* (2017), *The Malarkey* (2012) and *Glad of These Times* (2007). *Out of the Blue* was Helen Dunmore's selection drawing on her earlier Bloodaxe titles *Bestiary* (1997), *Recovering a Body* (1994), *Short Days, Long Nights: New & Selected Poems* (1991), *The Raw Garden* (1988), *The Sea Skater* (1986) and *The Apple Fall* (1983), as well as a new collection, *Out of the Blue*, and a selection of poems for children previously published in *Secrets* (Bodley Head, 1994). Fifteen poems which narrowly missed being included in *Out of the Blue* have been added to this edition; these are marked with asterisks in the contents listing.

Counting Backwards was Helen Dunmore's original title for *Inside the Wave*, which was first published in April 2017, with her final poem 'Hold out your arms' added to book's first reprint with her approval.

CONTENTS

Inside the Wave (2017)

19   Counting Backwards
20   The Underworld
21   Shutting the Gate
22   In Praise of the Piano
23   Re-opening the old mines
24   Inside the Wave
26   Odysseus to Elpenor
28   Plane tree outside Ward 78
29   The shaft
30   Leave the door open
31   My life's stem was cut
32   The Bare Leg
34   The Place of Ordinary Souls
35   My daughter as Penelope
37   The Lamplighter
38   The Halt
39   Bluebell Hollows
40   A Loose Curl
41   Hornsea, 1952
42   Festival of stone
43   A Bit of Love
44   Winter Balcony with Dunnocks
45   Mimosa
46   Nightfall in the IKEA Kitchen
48   The Duration
49   At the Spit
50   Terra Incognita
51   Four cormorants, one swan
52   Girl in the Blue Pool
53   February 12th 1994
54   What shall I do for my sister in the day she shall be spoken for?
55   In Secret
55   All the breaths of your life
56   Her children look for her
57   Little papoose

58   Cliffs of Fall
59   Five Versions from Catullus
59   1 *Through Babel of Nations*
59   2 *Undone*
59   3 *Sirmio*
60   4 *Dedication*
61   5 *Sparrow*
62   Rim
63   On looking through the handle of a cup
64   Ten Books
66   Subtraction
67   My people
68   September Rain

70   Hold out your arms

The Malarkey (2012)

75   The Malarkey
76   Come Out Now
78   The Inbox
79   Boatman
80   I Owned a Woman Once
82   *Longman English Series*
83   Writ in Water
88   Dis
89   Newgate
90   At Ease
91   Harbinger
91   The Hyacinths
92   The Night Workers
93   Agapanthus above Porthmeor
94   Visible and Invisible
94   The Snowfield
95   Lemon tree in November
96   Bildad
99   Skulking
99   Basement at Eighteen Folgate Street
100 Barclays Bank, St Ives
100 Playing Her Pieces
101 Pianist, 103,
102 The Torn Ship

103   Taken in Shadows

108   Prince Felipe Prospero (1657-1661)

108   Picture Messages

109   Lethe

110   The Queue's Essentially

110   The Captainess of Laundry

111   The Day's Umbrellas

112   The Deciphering

113   The Tarn

113   The Gift

114   What Will You Say

115   Cloud

115   I Have Been Thinking of You So Loudly

116   The Kingdom of the Dead

117   The Last Heartbeat

117   The Old Mastery

118   The Overcoat

118   Window Cleaners at Ladysmith Road

119   I Heard You Sing in the Dark

120   *La Recouvrance*

121   The Filament

Glad of These Times (2007)

125   City lilacs

126   Crossing the field

127   Litany

128   Don't count John among the dreams

129   The other side of the sky's dark room

129   Convolvulus

130   The grey lilo

131   Yellow butterflies

132   Plume

132   Odysseus

133   The blue garden

134   Violets

135   The rowan

136   Barnoon

137   Getting into the car

138   Glad of these times

140   Off-script

140   'Indeed we are all made from the dust of stars'

141 Tulip
142 Beautiful today the
143 Dead gull on Porthmeor
144 Narcissi
145 Dolphins whistling
147 Borrowed light
148 A winter imagination
149 Athletes
149 Pneumonia
150 Wall is the book
151 Gorse
152 Blackberries after Michaelmas
152 To my nine-year-old self
153 Fallen angel
154 Bridal
155 Still life with ironing
155 Spanish Irish
156 Cowboys
156 Below Hungerford Bridge
157 Ophelia
158 Winter bonfire
158 One A.M.
159 Lemon and stars
159 Cutting open the lemons
160 Hearing owls
161 'Often they go just before dawn'
162 May voyage

Out of the Blue (2001)

165 Out of the Blue
166 The man on the roof
167 Giraffes in Hull
168 Jacob's drum
169 That old cinema of memory
170 Depot
170 A lorry-load of stuff
172 Virgin with Two Cardigans
173 Ice coming
174 Cyclamen, blood-red
175 Piers Plowman: The Crucifixion & Harrowing of Hell
185 Smoke

186 Bristol Docks
188 The spill
189 Without remission
190 The rain's coming in
191 As good as it gets
192 If only
192 Mr Lear's ring
193 Fortune-teller on Church Road
194 Sleeveless
194 The point of not returning
195 The form
196 The sentence
196 With short, harsh breaths
197 The footfall
198 The coffin-makers
199 Inside out
200 The blessing

FROM *Bestiary* (1997)

203 Candle poem
204 At the Emporium
204 Next door
205 He lived next door all his life
206 Under the leaves*
207 The surgeon husband
208 Fishing beyond sunset
208 Hare in the snow
209 Need
211 Sometimes in the rough garden of city spaces
212 I should like to be buried in a summer forest
213 The scattering
214 All the things you are not yet
215 Ferns on a hospital window*
216 Diving girl
217 A pretty shape
218 Viking cat in the dark
219 Baby sleep
220 Frostbite
221 Basketball player on Pentecost Monday
222 Tiger lookout
223 Tiger Moth caterpillar

224   Hungry Thames

224   The wasp

225   On growing a black tulip *

226   Little Ellie and the timeshare salesman

227   Bouncing boy

227   Ghost at noon

228   Greek beads

229   Tea at Brandt's

230   We are men, not beasts

FROM *Recovering a Body* (1994)

233   To Virgil

234   Three Ways of Recovering a Body

236   Holiday to Lonely

237   Poem in a Hotel

238   The Bike Lane

239   Drink and the Devil

240   Ahvenanmaa

241   Rubbing Down the Horse

242   You came back to life in its sweetness

243   Heimat

244   In the Desert Knowing Nothing

245   Poem on the Obliteration of 100,000 Iraqi Soldiers

246   The Yellow Sky

247   Getting the Strap

248   Adders

249   The conception

250   Scan at 8 weeks

251   Pedalo

255   Beetroot Soup

256   The Diving Reflex

258   Bathing at Balnacarry

259   Boys on the Top Board

260   Sylvette Scrubbing

261   Babes in the Wood

262   Cajun

263   Then I think how the train *

264   Skips

264   Time by Accurist

265   The Silent Man in Waterstones

266   The Wardrobe Mistress

268   When You've Got
269   Afterword*

FROM *Secrets* (1994)

273   Lemon sole
274   Christmas caves
275   That violet-haired lady
276   Whooper swans
277   Snow Queen
278   The cuckoo game
279   The butcher's daughter
281   The greenfield ghost
282   Herring girl
283   Russian doll
284   Breeze of ghosts

FROM *Short Days, Long Nights* (1991)

287   Those shady girls
287   The dream-life of priests
289   Sisters leaving before the dance
291   On not writing certain poems
292   Privacy of rain
293   Dancing man
295   At Cabourg II
296   Baron Hardup
297   Nearly May Day
300   Three workmen with blue pails
301   Brown coal
303   Safe period
304   Big barbershop man
305   The dry well
306   Our family, swimming again*
307   Sweet pepper*
308   Heron
309   One yellow chicken
310   Sailing to Cuba
310   Off the West Pier
312   Winter 1955
313   Rinsing
313   To Betty, swimming

314   In Berber's Ice Cream Parlour
315   On drinking lime juice in September*
316   Not going to the forest
317   Lutherans

FROM *The Raw Garden* (1988)

321   Code-breaking in the Garden of Eden
323   Seal run
325   Wild strawberries
326   A mortgage on a pear tree
337   A pæony truss on Sussex place
328   Permafrost
329   At Cabourg
331   Ploughing the roughlands
332   The land pensions
333   A dream of wool
334   New crops
335   Shadows of my mother against a wall
336   Air layering
336   The argument
337   The peach house
338   A meditation of the glasshouses
339   The haunting of Epworth
340   Preaching at Gwennap
341   On circuit from Heptonstall Chapel
342   US 1st Division Airborne Ranger at rest in Honduras
343   One more for the beautiful table
344   Lambkin
344   Dublin 1971
346   The hard-hearted husband
348   Malta
349   Candlemas
349   Pilgrims
350   An Irish miner in Staffordshire

FROM *The Sea Skater* (1986)

353   The bride's nights in a strange village
354   Lazarus*
355   Christmas roses
356   I imagine you sent back from Africa

358   The knight*
359   In memoriam Cyril Smith 1913-1945
361   The parachute packers
363   Porpoise washed up on the beach
364   In deep water
365   Lady Macduff and the primroses
367   Mary Shelley
370   The plum tree
371   The air-blue gown
373   My sad descendants
374   Patrick at four years old on Bonfire Night
375   The horse landscape
376   Thetis
377   In the tents
378   Uncle Will's telegram
379   Rapunzel
381   Bewick's swans*
382   The sea skater
383   In the tea house
384   Florence in permafrost
386   Missile launcher passing at night

FROM *The Apple Fall* (1983)

389   The marshalling yard
390   A cow here in the June meadow
391   Zelda
392   Annunciation off East Street*
393   The Polish husband
395   The damson
396   In Rodmell Garden
397   The apple fall
398   Pictures of a Chinese nursery*
399   Pharaoh's daughter
400   Domestic poem
401   Patrick I
402   Patrick II
403   Weaning
403   Clinic day*
404   Approaches to winter
406   The night chemist
407   St Paul's

408   Poem for December 28
409   Greenham Common
410   Poem for hidden women
412   If no revolution come
414   A safe light
415   Near Dawlish
415   The last day of the exhausted month
416   Second marriages*
417   The deserted table
418   The writer's son
419   Ollie and Charles at St Andrew's Park
420   Winter fairs
420   In a wood near Turku
421   Landscape from the Monet Exhibition at Cardiff
422   Breakfast

423   INDEX OF TITLES AND FIRST LINES

Inside the Wave

(2017)

for Susan Glickman

Counting Backwards

Untroubled, the anaesthetist
Potters with his cannula
As the waterfall in the ante-room
Grows steadily louder,

All of them are cool with it
And just keep on working
No wonder they wear Wellingtons –
I want to ask them

But it seems stupid, naive,
Even attention-seeking.
Basalt, I think, the rock
Where the white stream leaps.

Imagine living at such volume
Next door to a waterfall,
Stepping in and out of the noise
In their funny clothes.

But you can get used to anything
Like the anaesthetist
Counting to himself
Backwards, all wrong.

The Underworld

And besides, we might play cards:
Those slapdash games you once taught me
Which any fool can remember
Or from the fabric which has been tied
With string, wrapped in brown paper
Put away in the highest cupboard
Since the time the children were young
And everyone's children were young
I might make new curtains
And hem them all by hand.

I used to be so afraid of failing
To grasp the moment, the undertone,
To look foolish in the eyes of anyone
But now I like the patter of cards
The lazy sandwich that falls open
Halfway to the mouth,
The refills in a thumbed glass
The way people get up, yawn,
Go stiff-legged to the window, wondering
That it isn't yet tomorrow

It's a long way from here to the river:
I like to see the fish come in
But the game is still on.
From the way the cards are falling
I'd say you will win.
I used to think it was a narrow road
From here to the underworld
But it's as broad as the sun.
I say to you: I have more acquaintance
Among the dead than the living
And I am not pretending.
It's pure fact, like this sandwich
Which hasn't quite tempted anyone.

Shutting the Gate

A barefoot girl hugs the wall
On tiptoe, her instep
Arched like a cat's back.
Nearby a car revs.
She looks at me and smiles
Like a primary-school child.
Her friend smokes by the gate
One hand on the wall.
Lissom as lilies, they shake dark curls
And watch the car.

I say: Are you girls all right?
And she says: We don't like
The look of them. Two men
In the dark of the car, also smoking.
She swings the gate shut.
They might be my daughters –
A little older, I reckon –
But those men don't look
Much like the sons of anyone.

It's late, almost two A.M.
They are both inside the gate
With one shoe-strap broken
A packet of cigarettes
Brief lovely dresses.
I ask: Will you be all right?
They don't want to come inside,
They just didn't like the gate open
When those men were waiting
Like that, with the engine going
And from time to time a rev
So we don't forget.

In Praise of the Piano

In praise of the piano that slips out of tune
I raise my needle from the dusty record
And watch the vinyl turn and turn,

In praise of the unrepeatable, the original,
The one thought clinging to the one word
I dip my nib into the inkwell,

In praise of the only known photograph
Of your great-grandmother, I hoard
Film, blackout, developing bath.

O needle jumping on dusty vinyl
O letter stuffed in dirty pigeonhole
The fragile, the original
The one word before the blot falls.

Finger ballet on the telephone switchboard,
The one word that flows from the lips
And the one heart by which it is heard

Unrepeatable, fragile. In praise
Of all that cleaves to the note, then slips
From it, and never stays.

Re-opening the old mines

But you would have to go below
The bare bright surface. And I suppose
Out of the dark would come marching
Men with tattoos
Of dust on their forearms,
And as for the gorse burning its own fuse
Or the boy who drops to his knees

Shuffling along his seam
Towards the pock of an explosion
Heard from above, miles out
In the fishing grounds,
He's in the shop, serving
Eighty flavours of ice cream.
Drip drip goes brown water
Into the shaft while harebells quiver.

Under the houses there's a cavern
So deep that when the camera
Was lowered it swung pendulum
While the void kept opening
But I suppose that in the veiny dark
Tunnels that knit the rock
They are still blasting,
And ponies which never see the light
Snuff sugar and are content

As may be among the rare metals:
Antimony, molybdenum,
Wolframite, uranium
Gold, silver and indium.

Inside the Wave

And when at last the voyage was over
The ship docked and the men paid off,
The crew became a scattering
Dotted, unremarkable,
In houses along the hill top
Where the lamps flared in welcome
And then grew dim, where a woman turned
As if from habit to the wall.

In the bronze mirror there was a woman
Combing what was left of her hair
And beside her, grimacing,
A dirty old mariner.
He swore and knocked back the chair.

Yes, then Odysseus opened his mouth
And all that was left
Was the sound an old man makes
Between a laugh and a cough.
His toenails were goat's hooves
His hair a wild
Nest of old stories,

He straddled the tiles
As a man of the sea does
But she would not touch
His barnacled lips.
From the fountain, pulse by pulse
Came gouts of blood.

Everything stayed as it was,
There was no unravelling
Of wake behind him,
No abandoning
Unwanted memories and men.
Besides, the earth stank.

He went down to the black rock
Where the sea pours
And the white sand blows,
He turned his back to the land
And thought of nothing
For the voyage was over,
The ship dragged by a chain
Onto the ramp for inspection.

The waves turned and turned
Neither toward nor away from him,
Swash and backwash
Crossing, repeating,
But never the same.
At the lip of the wave, foam
Stuttered and broke,

It was on the inside
Of the wave he chose
To meditate endlessly
Without words or song,
And so he lay down
To watch it at eye-level,
About to topple
About to be whole.

Odysseus to Elpenor

But tell me, Elpenor
Now that I have conjured you
From those caverns so deep
No camera can fathom them

Now you have come to drink the wine
Poured on the ground in libation
And slake your fleshless appetite
On the snuff of blood,

Tell me how you came here
Fleeing like a cloud shadow
Over restless water –
You frighten me, Elpenor.

Look, I have drawn my sword
Are you not afraid?
You were a handsome fighter –
Will you come on?

Take the heat of my hand
Elpenor, between your palms.
Bow your head for a blessing
Houseless boy, and now tell me

How you came to die.
We are not heroes, any of us,
Only familiars
Of grey shores and the sea-pulse,

Laggards, like the tide.
Was it you, Elpenor
Who rowed when the wind died
Until your hands bled?

You fell asleep in Circe's house
Drunk, like all of us,
Playing the fool
As you plunged from the roof.

When your neck broke
We were already racing
Down to the harbour
Where our black ship quivered,

Even when our sails filled
And we scudded before the wind
We could not catch your shadow.
We had left you behind

But you are ahead of us
Waiting, unpropitiated
Poor boy, unburied
Come to lap at the blood.

Dawn pushes away night's curtain
Your body must be burned
And your hair tied with ribbons
As a remembrance.

You ask me in the name of my son
Not to let you be forgotten
But to build your grave mound
Where the pebbles meet the tide

'And thrust into its heart my oar
So that I may row myself forever.'

Plane tree outside Ward 78

The tree outside the window
Is lost and gone,
Billow of leaf in the summer dark,
A buffet of rain.

I might owe this tree to morphine,
I might wake in the morning
To find it dissolved, paper
Hung in water,

Nothing to do with dreams.
I cannot sleep.
Pain is yards away
Held off like bad weather,

In the ward's beautiful contentment
Freed by opiates.
Hooked to oxygen
We live for the moment.

The shaft

I don't need to go to the sun –
It lies on my pillow.

Without movement or speech
Day deepens its sweetness.

Sea shanties from the water,
A brush of traffic,

But it's quiet here.
Who would have thought that pain

And weakness had such gifts
Hidden in their rough hearts?

Leave the door open

Leave the door open! We cheep and command
From the shared double bed or from the cot
With bars that make tigers out of the dark.
We want the fume and coil of your cigarettes,
The smoke that has embraced us from birth,

The click of your footsteps on the wooden landing,
The wedge of light that parts us from the dark
As I hold, hold to it like a sword.
Leave the door open. Go downstairs, go out
After priming the neighbours to listen,

Go to your world: the cider-bottle cap
Askew on its stem, the pellucid gin,
The ashtray overflowing with stubs,
Radio laughter and suppressed voices
As you creak upstairs without waking us,

But don't forget to leave the light on
So the spill of it falls where it must.
We can breathe now in our coffin of sheets
So tangled we can't get out of them,
As long as you leave the door open.

My life's stem was cut

My life's stem was cut,
But quickly, lovingly
I was lifted up,
I heard the rush of the tap
And I was set in water
In the blue vase, beautiful
In lip and curve,
And here I am
Opening one petal
As the tea cools.
I wait while the sun moves
And the bees finish their dancing,
I know I am dying
But why not keep flowering
As long as I can
From my cut stem?

The Bare Leg

There we sat in the clattering dark
As the carriages swayed downhill
Under London's invisible rivers,
There our faces were mute
With a day of burdens
As we recovered ourselves,

Some read star signs from a column
In a left-behind newspaper,
Some sighed and shut their eyes.
When the train came to a halt
For nothing in the dark of the tunnel
We breathed out silence

And when the voice came
Lulling with news of a red signal
We sighed again and rolled our eyes
Or adjusted our standing positions
To lean into one another more gently

And if we had room to turn our heads
We looked down the long corridor
Of carriages aligned
As if the driver had drawn them
Onto the straight, and left them perfect

And in the next-to-one carriage
Less crowded than our own
A bare leg stretched into the aisle
Taking up room
As if this were a beach in summer.

We studied the delicate anatomy
Of shin and knee
The putting together and planting
Of toe and heel
The tension of thigh,

And beyond it nothing
For the body was hidden
By the bulk of a boy
Inopportunely leaning
To adjust his headphones.

As if this were a beach in summer
The leg took its own time
And flexed luxuriously
While the signal held against us
And delay surged into time

Lost, irrecoverable.
The driver told us again
We would be on the move shortly
But no one believed him.
This was what we had always known

Was about to happen: the calf tightening
The vessel of the hip cupping
The thrust of the bare leg,
The naked precision of the human
As it steps into action,

And down the long corridor, swaying
As the train resumed,
The chant, the murmur
Of foot soles, someone
Merely walking into the next room.

The Place of Ordinary Souls

In such meadows the days pass
Without shadow, unremarkable.
On time, the bus pants at its halt,
Passengers peel their thighs
From hot vinyl, and step down.

Swift-heeled Achilles strides
Through the fields of asphodel
Flanked by heroes and warriors
Who have left their mark on the earth
And want nothing to do with us.

With impatient glance at the starry fields
And kit on their backs, they're gone
Route-marching to Elysium
Where the gods are at home.
We are glad to see the back of them.

In the fields of asphodel we dawdle
Towards the rumour of a beauty spot
Which turns out to be shut.
No matter. Why not get out the picnic
And see if the tea's still hot?

The bus shuttles all day long
With its cargo of ordinary souls.
We lie on our backs, eyes closed,
Dreaming of nothing while clouds pass.

(According to Greek legend, ordinary, unheroic souls pass the afterlife
in the fields of asphodel.)

My daughter as Penelope

Seven years old last birthday,
With waist-length hair,
White tunic, yellow ribbon
Threaded at neck and hem,

She has learned her lines,
The chalked-in positions,
The music which means
She must come out of the wings.

In the dusty cave of the theatre
The children's bare feet patter.
My daughter thrusts out her arm
And beats her suitors,

In pride at the laughter
She forgets the pause,
But chides them, berates them
Like an abandoned woman

Who has over cold years learned
To preserve the hearth.
Odysseus, so long expected
Would scarcely be welcome –

A man of many distractions
At this very moment
Oblivious of her
Conjuring the dead with blood.

My daughter as Penelope
Shakes back her hair and cries
That they should all go home
Here they will get nothing,

While the little capering boys
Evade her blows.

I made her tunic, I threaded
Those ribbons at neck and hem,
I brushed and loosened her hair.
She leaned against my shoulder

In pure naïvety. 'I didn't know
You could make anything
As good as this,' she said.
The theatre swallowed the child.

We thought they were too young for it,
They would freeze, or be afraid,
But they were blithe, barefoot,
Running from the underworld

To butt like kids against the white sheet
That marked the kingdom of the dead.
The skin rose on our arms
The hairs prickled. They'd gone.

My daughter as Penelope
Seven years old, thrusting
Her bare arm out of her chiton
Pushing away her suitors

As one may do in childhood.
The sheet quivered
For the dead could barely contain
Their desire for the living

And the play was long.
The cave of the stage grew vast –
A mouth without a tongue
Consuming our children.

The Lamplighter

Here, where the old Industrial School was
And then the porn-film sheds,
Stands the last lamp before the water.
Dead as he's been these ninety years
The lamplighter on his beat
Walks with ladder on shoulder.
Above the Mardyke Steps and the donkey track
He fixes ladder to pole, stands back
Then climbs nimbly into the mass of flower.
His head is a ball of petals. He barely coughs
As the soft skin of petunia
Plasters itself against his nostrils.

Now he takes up his torch
Tips the lever and touches the gas.
A big rude flower, a dahlia
Blooms in its case.
There are boys slouched against the wall
Up to no good, there are white-faced girls
Running to the shop for a paper of chips.
There's the long fall of the Mardyke Steps
Tunneling the bad way to the docks
And so the lamplighters muster
To stop the thieves who can knock you down
Between one lamp and the next,
Between one step and the drop.

The Halt

We stop somewhere on the plain
While I am sleeping. As my book slips
The man opposite leans to stop it
Still chomping that sausage he cut
With a penknife opened and cleaned
On his sleeve, long before I slept.

He pulls down the window-strap and at once
We hear birds scurry in the scrub
That bows and knits to the cuff of the wind.
I turn my face to the glass
For I speak his language painfully
Sentence by sentence, and he will talk to me.

We have halted for no reason
In the white glare of noon
At this shack surrounded by sunflowers
Pothering hens and a plot of maize
Beyond which the land gallops unbroken.
There is also a woman

Who swings a bucket on her arm
As she clambers the makeshift platform
Box upon box, skilfully placed.
She knows all the long curve of the train.
Now from the engine a stoker swings
A stream of water that dings on the iron.

The rails flash so I can barely look at them.
Our engine shucks steam as it canters
Panting, pulling against the brake.
The bucket clangs. The woman steps down.
From my sticky mouth the words come:
Hens, maize, sunflowers,
Her bowed head and the way she waits.

Bluebell Hollows

Are they blue or not blue?
All I know is the smoke
That moves under the trees,

In Tremenheere Woods
Moths clung to the sheet,
It was the hour of innocence –

We developed flowers
On light-sensitive paper:
They are still here.

We could never walk fast enough,
Seven year olds
Up in the dead of night

Climbing to the lookout
Where bonfires blazed
For reasons long forgotten,

But perhaps because the Romans
Once came this far
To walk the bluebell hollows.

A Loose Curl

I have never known you easily
Hold my hand as you do now.
We sit here for hours.

There's salt all over the glass
And however I look to the horizon
Not a sail to be seen.

I hold your hand and say nothing.
Once I must have held
Your finger, a loose curl.

You remember in snatches.
You say you're afraid of a whale
Snorkelling through the blue Arctic.

The ice is so fragile.
You must spread your weight, like this
And inch out to the abyss.

This is not a glacier, it's only
A world of ice falling apart.
I think something is moving slowly

Deep in your fingers.
The sea stays in its lair
But wants to be where we are.

Hornsea, 1952

... I by the tide
Of Humber would complain...

Yes, but were we happy then?
The wind blew from the east, you were always cold,
And there was a boating lake –
Water trapped on your left, below sea level,
Murkily waiting to be stirred by boys with sticks.

You and I must have been conspirators
All those cold days. The two of us.
No books, no essays, no bike propped up
In happy rush. No clangour of bells
Or notes in pigeon-holes:
I can't wait for you, my darling.

Huge planes take off
Overhead into loneliness,
You bake sponge cakes at four o'clock
For belated homecomings –
Men drink in the Mess.

The fortune-teller saw you kneel
Beside your trunk, packing, unpacking.
The hour for scholarship came round again:
You won. You win
And write Oxford on labels
Flowingly, beneath your name.

A small child drags at your hand.
Another pushes out your belly-button.
You haul at the pram.
The two of us. How the wind blows.
You lose one child and you keep one.
You will change your accent for no one.

41

You could write an essay on this:
A sozzled officer slow to come home,
Marvell's vegetable kingdom,
World enough and time,
Another baby fattening
And your thirtieth birthday on the horizon.

Festival of stone

(for Jitka Palmer)

The chink of hammers is a song
Like blackbirds interrupted, alarming
One another in the beauty of the morning

Over the thud of mallets, raspings on stone
As the sculptors bend and sweat
And the skirts of the tents blow out.

The chink of hammers is the wind that plays
On plane leaves keyed to a ripple
In the updraught from the water

And all is flash and shatter
As the surface breaks open
To show the face of the stone.

A Bit of Love

He must stir himself. No more hiding
Behind the skill of hands
That are not his.

Those nurses are good girls.
They'll do anything for you –
Within reason of course.

He must fumble his old fingers
Get himself moving –
They all say this.

Ambulance bells carouse
Until he doesn't know where he is.
Drunks in the street

Swaying about like Holy Moses
That's about the size of it:
No one listens.

The lamplighter went home years ago
There's no night policeman
Or dawn milk-chink.

That stout world is a trinket
In the eyes of his grandchildren.
His shifts are over.

Here's a bit of paper
And a book to lean on
What more does he want?

In his well-taught hand-writing
He'll send her a bit of love
To make her blush.

Winter Balcony with Dunnocks

Close to the earth, creeping, lowly
Mouse-coloured, unglamorous
Dunnocks, your dusty wings flirt
In the dry roots of ivy, you are unnoted
Untweeted creatures, you turn
Dry leaves and peck for grubs.

You come to my balcony, a cloud of you
Eight floors up and slender-dark
Tilting your wings to skirt the railing
And flicker among the geraniums
As the winter cold comes on –
Quick, quick, against the dusk.

You don't care that someone was here
Before you: those two fat pigeons
Dumpily purring, the noisy ones
Who think I can't see where they slump
Between flower-pot and plastic bucket
Breast to breast, at roost –

No, you are too quick-dark
On the rim of night, flickering
Through the chill buds of the camellia,
Unnoted, untweeted creatures,
Dunnocks, foraging
December and the year's husk.

Mimosa

Why is the mimosa here
Inside its dark frame?

So down-to-earth, it comes out workmanlike
Year after year, breaks its own branches
With plumes that make the sky quiver.

Let's sit here, on the bench, under it
To rest while you get your breath.

Winter's over, and look, in this dustbin
Someone has planted wallflowers.
There's pollen all over your arms.

Nightfall in the IKEA Kitchen

Nightfall in the IKEA kitchen.
Even though the lights are left on
I feel the push of the wind's deconstruction
Take the hull of the shed by storm.

Creak and strain of test and fault-finding
But here in the glow I am alone
Expected and consoled. Here is the notice board
Riddled with reminders and invitations,

Here are picture ledges and high cabinets
Kitchen trolley, drying racks
A sly shoe cabinet, fabric pocket-ties:
A life so sweetly cupboarded

I barely believe it is mine. Open
And another light comes on.
Here is the place where I begin again
As a twenty-three year old Finn

Taking the keys of her first home.
I use space well here. I waste nothing.
The floor clock has shelves, the bed lifts up
And if I yield and sleep

I will become part of the storage system
Harbouring dreams and heat.
Everything is a little below scale
And therefore ample. Stuva, Dröma

Expedit, Tromsø, Isfjorden...
I rock in the peace of their names
Even as I mispronounce them
For this is nightfall in the one-bedroom

Model apartment's kitchen
When everyone has gone home
And there is nothing left
But the Marketplace itself.

And say a child is born, no problem.
With a simple room-divider
I can create not only child storage
But also a home office

From which I will provide for us both.
Look, here is his football on the floor
And here a shelf where it may be stored.
His whole life is in these drawers.

Call him Billy and see him run.
When he grows up and moves out
Just take down the partition
To have, at last, my own space again.

Ten thousand times the wind has pushed the doors
But they have not opened yet.
Those cupboards. Stockholm. Yes, that green
Nature can never quite get.

The Duration

Here they are on the beach where the boy played
For fifteen summers, before he grew too old
For French cricket, shrimping and rock pools.

Here is the place where he built his dam
Year after year. See, the stream still comes down
Just as it did, and spreads itself on the sand

Into a dozen channels. How he enlisted them:
Those splendid spades, those sun-bonneted girls
Furiously shoring up the ramparts.

Here they are on the beach, just as they were
Those fifteen summers. She has a rough towel
Ready for him. The boy was always last out of the water.

She would rub him down hard, chafe him like a foal
Up on its legs for an hour and trembling, all angles.
She would dry carefully between his toes.

Here they are on the beach, the two of them
Sitting on the same square of mackintosh,
The same tartan rug. Quality lasts.

There are children in the water, and mothers patrolling
The sea's edge, calling them back
From the danger zone beyond the breakers.

How her heart would stab when he went too far out.
Once she flustered into the water, shouting
Until he swam back. He was ashamed of her then.

Wouldn't speak, wouldn't look at her even.
Her skirt was sopped. She had to wring out the hem.
She wonders if Father remembers.

Later, when they've had their sandwiches
She might speak of it. There are hours yet.
Thousands, by her reckoning.

At the Spit

If you lie down at the Spit on this warm
But sunless afternoon, here on the pebbles,
Smelling the wrack and sea-blown plastic,
If you squint at the clouds that sag on the horizon
Without bringing rain or allowing the sun,
If you lie down here in the hollow
And take your backpack for a pillow
And watch how the pebbles lose colour
And then, shutting your eyes, listen,
You'll hear the tide swell and the wrack dry
To fool's balloons, incurably saline
Crackling under the weight of your backpack
As you lie down,

If you lie down and as they say do nothing
You'll hear the tongue of the tide licking
The Spit – O fine appetite! – You'll hear the click
And tumble of pebbles, slumbrous
Geography shifting: this is the land mass
And this the plastic, the wrack, the mess
To pick over in search of a home. Go back,
It's late and the unseen sun's dropping
Hurts the clouds and turns them to rain.
Drowsy, at home, you lie and dream
Of longboats and long-shed blood
Of corner shops and running for sweets –
O sweet familiarity, geography
Melting into the known –

Terra Incognita

And now we come to the unknown land
With its blue coves and inlets where sweet water
Bubbles against the salt. Its sand
Is ready for footprints. Give me your hand

Onto the rock where the seaweed clings
And the red anemone throbs in its crevice
Through swash and backwash. These things
Various as the brain's comb and the tide's swing

Or the first touch of untouched terrain
On our footsoles, as the land explores us,
Have become our fortune. Let me explain
Which foods are good to eat, and which poison.

Four cormorants, one swan

The swans go up with slow wing-beats
That strike off from the surface of the water.
Even the most absorbed games-player
Deep in his mobile, looks up at the clatter
Of six swans' wings.

After the swans have patrolled their harbour
They settle singly. One drifts with the current
To the house-boat window that always opens,
Another sails towards two cormorants
Hanging out their wings

And two coosing, or fishing
In the shallows beside the jetty.
Now the whole afternoon hangs
In the balance between four cormorants
And a single swan, approaching.

The first cormorant pratfalls from its perch
In an ungainly bundle of wings
Or so it seems. But no, it is flying
Arrowlike to a fish a hundred yards off.
A lover could not be more direct.

Girl in the Blue Pool

Years back and full of echoes.
Chlorine, urine, raucous
Cuff of voices on broken surface.
A boy on the edge rowdily teeters
And you, knees flexed, arms back
Are on the pulse of your stroke. Suppose
It is you, now, in the pink bikini, close
To making five hundred metres
As the ceiling splinters with echoes.

Suppose you touch the tiles on the turn
And vanish. The churn
Of bubbles streams at your heels
While you shake water out of your ears
To catch the voice of your instructor
Who paces you, outpaces you
On the blue-wet tiles. How her voice echoes.
You should not be wearing a bikini
And you were slow on the turn.

I am years back and full of echoes.
The silver stream where you swim
Has long ago been swallowed,
But at your temples the lovely hollows
Play in June light. Suppose
There is one length left in you, knees flexed
Arms back. Chlorine, urine, raucous
Voices on shattered surface. If that boy topples
You too will go down.

February 12th 1994

No one else remembers that room
With the blood pressure cuff and the plastic cot
And the bag on its stand dripping
Millilitre by millilitre
When the visitors had gone home
And the tyres six storeys down
Skidded, infrequent.

Snow on the window ticked
The glass, becoming sleet
And the sheets for all their stains were white.
No one else remembers that room
Where you cried each time the lights
Went off and the nurses were absent
For hours by morphia time,

I reached for you in pain
And lifted you in your hospital nightgown
To wedge you against me
For we were both falling
You with purple, dangling limbs
Ecstatic, all lips
And quick, hot breathing,

I watching a nurse who did not exist
Write her hieroglyphics
As the snow thickened.
I made a vow to you then
In our solitude
That you would never remember,
With two fingers I smoothed the ruck
Of the gown against your back.

What shall I do for my sister in the day she shall be spoken for?

I have a little sister, she has no breasts.
I buy her face covering at the shop
Where they have nearly run out.
So, we are lucky. Black cloth sucks
Into her nostrils. My sister screams.

When she's finished saying she can't breathe
When I've cleaned the snot from her face
And rearranged her so she'll be safe
I say: It's for your own good.
Do as I do and walk close.

I have a little sister, she has no breasts.
She would like to be an ophthalmologist.
When she was three she had a cyst
Removed from under her left eyelid.
I say: Don't cry, you can still see out.

I tell her to walk between me and the wall
And keep her eyes downward. We scuttle
Like crabs in a black wrapping.
We shall buy rice, we shall go home.
What shall I do for my sister
In the day when she shall be spoken for?

In Secret

And this is where they met in secret.
Follow my pointing finger. Now you see it
Quite empty. Those curtains that veiled it

Are rags, and the bed stripped bare.
Here she played for him, there
He placed his shoes in the corner.

Piano from an upstairs room,
Wanton extravagance of scales falling
As we imagine birdsong –

But only slow it down
And hear the gong-repeat of a rhythm
Like the treading of rubble over a woman.

All the breaths of your life

There is a gargoyle look when the mouth caves.
No more words can be hoped for, the lips
Are not for speaking, the tongue
Is all sag and distortion.

I might think that your kindness is effaced.
No more look can be hoped for, your eyes
Are not for seeing, the skin
Is a drawn curtain over them.

I hear your breath, now failing
As all the breaths of your life become
Petals endlessly opening
Inward, where the dark is.

Her children look for her

Life and death are in the hands of God she said
As a boat is in the hands of the dark water,

And now her children look for her
In the zizz of her sewing-machine each evening
And the smell of cardamom.

She said: life and death are in the hands of God.
As the sun beat on the roof of the van
She closed her eyes to dream,

And her children look as the Pole Star goes up
Close to the moon.

Little papoose

If I were the moon
With a star papoose
In the windy sky
I'd carry my one star home,

If I were the sea
With boats in my arms
On this cold morning
I'd carry them,

If I were sleeping
And my dream turned
I would carry you
Little papoose
Wherever you choose.

Cliffs of Fall

(to the memory of Gerard Manley Hopkins)

Spring of turf and thrift, tangle of fleece, sheep-shit,
Subtle flowers where honeybees knock
At the foxglove lip and the gorse trap

Then sheer on our left the drop. Spatter of bracken hooks
Misleading the lambs. In the bank, marsh violets
Wet, lovely, minute. We need not look for the fall, the chink

Of pebble that tumbles. All the grey scree stirs
Slip-rattles and stills itself. Here is the slope's
Angle, implacable. Here's where you look

Touch, unbalance, dislodge. Infinite drop
Where the bee burrs at the foxglove's lip,
All quick-tongued, intimate.

Time to step back to the wide margin
Cleave to the path's dapper attention
Unspring each poem,

Pitch each new note to the key of loss,
Lose nothing. Stay clear of the drop
Where the world bursts through its dirty glass.

Sun on your neck, a dazzle of violets
Infinitely slipsliding –
No quick wing-beat of flight, but a slope

Of gravel-rubble, its angle implacable
stripping you raw. From here your fall
Is a matter of form: a slow marvel.

Five Versions from Catullus

1 *Through Babel of Nations*

Through babel of nations and waste of water
I come my brother. What are these rites to us?
Your ashes are speechless
My words falter.

Blind fate has taken you, brother,
You and I are undone.
The wine I bring you is spoiled
With the salt of parting –
What else can I give?
Only a last greeting.

2 *Undone*

What you have done to me has undone me.
You have led me so far from myself
That my mind loses its bearings.
Even if you shape-shifted
To your best and dearest
I couldn't care for it. Dark love drives me on.

3 *Sirmio*

Almost island and jewel of all islands
In lakes stiller than thought or in wild oceans
Sweet or salt as the sea-god makes them,
Sirmio,

I see you, all of you, I take you in
I see you, barely believing
I've left those featureless, endless Bithynian plains.

We travel over many waters
To reach home-coming,
Struggle and suffering over, the mind dissolved
Of all its troubles, burdens laid down –
The soft bed waits for our exhaustion.

I see you, all of you, I know your
Confusion of ripples against the lakeshore
Welcoming laughter
The sounds of home
Ringing like masts in harbour:
Sirmio.

4 *Dedication*

My slim volume, polished almost to nothing –
Shall I dedicate it to you, Cornelius?

You thought something of my songs
Even though you were the only man in Italy

Who could wrap up the world in three tomes
Of flawless erudition.

My God, your learning and labour
Lean heavily against my little volume,

So take my book, this fingernail's width
For what it's worth.

5 *Sparrow*

Sparrow, my girl's delight
And plaything held to her breast,
Sparrow whom she teases with one finger
Daring your littleness to peck harder –
Sparrow, I burn for her
And crave the smallest crumb
As the pair of you play
Folded together in rapture
Under one wing.
I too long to comfort her
In grief or oppressive longing –
If only I could play with her as you do
Until she forgets her soul's sadness.

Rim

Here is the bowl. Do I want it still
Chipped as it is and crazed,
Its lustrous cream no longer running
Over the body in fleet glaze,

I'm getting rid, getting shot, cleansing
Dark cupboards and fossil-deep
Drawers lined with historic newspaper.
I stop to read about the three-day-week.

Here are gewgaws with tarnished clasps
Here is the gravy-boat, the one item
Surviving from the wedding service.
Here's Ted Heath's improbable grin.

I flick the rim and it gives back a tang –
Yes, I remember that, the exact sound
Of early curiosity and boredom.
Bowl on my palm, I twist it round

And round again, unsure.
Do I hold or let it fall?

On looking through the handle of a cup

On looking through the handle of a cup
I spied a nest of green: the spout
Minus the can, a bunch of leaves
Big as my hand: two trees
In the palm of the wind,

On looking through the hole made by a pin
In a plane leaf twirled
All ways to catch the world
I saw a drop of rain, swollen
On the petal of a rose,

On looking through the fault in my eyes
With their arrhythmias of vision
I saw what no one has seen:
My cup-handle of a world,
My pinhole morning.

Ten Books

Jacketless, buckled, pressed from the voyage,
Ten books that once were crated to America
And back again,
That have known the salt sea's swing under them,
Oil stink, the deep throb of the engines
And quick hands putting them back on the shelves.

Spines torn, the paper wartime, the Faber
Font squarish and the dates in Roman:
The Waste Land and other poems,
Poems Newly Selected, Siegfried Sassoon –
How that name conjured with me
As a soldier kicked at a dead man.

MacNeice, freckled with brown
From many damps in many different houses.
On the inner page, under my father's autograph
An early flourish of blue crayon
Where I scribbled a figure so primitive
There are not even legs for it to walk upon.

Bowed, chipped, darkening, edge-worn
Sunned, loose, fading
Binding copy, reading copy, shaken:
Ten books that I have taken.
From the balcony on an August morning
I see the rest fly to the tip lorry

Where the sofa for a moment reposes
Legs in the air, grinning.
It is soaked through with music
But nothing will save it.
Behind it the sea makes the usual silveriness,
The café opens and the bikes whizz

From end to end of the promenade.
Meanwhile in my father's hand, a quotation
On the title page of Herbert Read's
Thirty-Five Poems: 'I absorbed Blake,
His strange beauty, his profound message,
His miraculous technique, and to emulate

Blake was to be my ambition
And my despair...' (Faber and Faber,
24 Russell Square.) I see my own hands
Smooth and small as they are not now
Lifting, turning, 'I am amazed
To find how much I owe to him.'

Subtraction

You always thought that you'd die mid-stride,
Sun on your left hand, darkness
Crossing you out in one swipe.

When you got on to subtraction
It was easy-peasy. Add one
At the top, take one from the next column.

Good at take-away, good at adding,
Revving up for the 11-plus
But no mathematician,

You stumbled upon infinity
With infinite terror, and knew
The limits of divinity –

What you'd been told was wrong.
If all you loved had been given
Then all could be taken.

You knew then that you must blot
In the blue notebook, trim
With happy pencil, the sum
Of what is when it is not.

My people

My people are the dying,
I am of their company
And they are mine,
We wake in the wan hour
Between three and four,
Listen to the rain
And consider our painkillers.
I lie here in the warm
With four pillows, a light
And the comfort of my phone
On which I sometimes compose,
And the words come easily
Bubbling like notes
From a bird that thinks it is dawn.

My people are the dying.
I reach out to them,
A company of suffering.
One falls by the roadside
And a boot stamps on him,
One lies in her cell, alone,
Without tenderness
Brutally handled
Towards her execution.
I can do nothing.
This is my vigil: the lit candle,
The pain, the breath of my people
Drawn in pain.

September Rain

Always rain, September rain,
The slipstream of the season,
Night of the equinox, the change.

There are three surfers out back.
Now the rain's pulse is doubled, the wave
Is not to be caught. Are they lost in the dark

Do they know where the coast is combed with light
Or is there only the swell, lifting
Back to the beginning

When they ran down the hill like children
Through this rain, September rain,
And the sea opened its breast to them?

I lie and listen
And the life in me stirs like a tide
That knows when it must be gone.

I am on the deep deep water
Lightly held by one ankle
Out of my depth, waiting.

Hold out your arms

Death, hold out your arms for me
Embrace me
Give me your motherly caress,
Through all this suffering
You have not forgotten me.

You are the bearded iris that bakes its rhizomes
Beside the wall,
Your scent flushes with loveliness,
Sherbet, pure iris
Lovely and intricate.

I am the child who stands by the wall
Not much taller than the iris.
The sun covers me
The day waits for me
In my funny dress.

Death, you heap into my arms
A basket of unripe damsons
Red crisscross straps that button behind me.
I don't know about school,
My knowledge is for papery bud covers
Tall stems and brown
Bees touching here and there, delicately
Before a swerve to the sun.

Death stoops over me
Her long skirts slide,
She knows I am shy.
Even the puffed sleeves on my white blouse
Embarrass me,
She will pick me up and hold me
So no one can see me,
I will scrub my hair into hers.

There, the iris increases
Note by note
As the wall gives back heat.
Death, there's no need to ask:
A mother will always lift a child
As a rhizome
Must lift up a flower
So you settle me
My arms twining,
Thighs gripping your hips
Where the swell of you is.

As you push back my hair
– Which could do with a comb
But never mind –
You murmur
'We're nearly there.'

(25 May 2017)

71

The Malarkey

(2012)

...the most beautiful thing on this dark earth...

SAPPHO

The Malarkey

Why did you tell them to be quiet
and sit up straight until you came back?
The malarkey would have led you to them.

You go from one parked car to another
and peer through the misted windows
before checking the registration.

Your pocket bulges. You've bought them sweets
but the mist is on the inside of the windows.
How many children are breathing?

The malarkey's over in the back of the car.
The day is over outside the windows.
No street light has come on.

You fed them cockles soused in vinegar,
you took them on the machines.
You looked away just once.

You looked away just once
as you leaned on the chip-shop counter,
and forty years were gone.

You have been telling them for ever
Stop that malarkey in the back there!
Now they have gone and done it.
Is that mist, or water with breath in it?

Come Out Now

Come out now and stand beside me,
grasp the rail as the swell lifts you
above this inky, innocent city

which has put away all but the whoop of an ambulance
quickly suppressed, all but the chain of lights
slung westward across the Mendips,

all but the last cry of a drunk by the docks,
the salt taste of a locked-out tide,
the clipping hooves of a police horse.

Come out now and stand beside me.
I promise I won't look
and won't breathe in too deeply

the first smoke from the cigarette
you have naturally lit.

Here are only things you love.
Look to your left, where the *Matthew*
rears its cargo of flags,

or where masts chink in the dark
and a rat pours down a rope
from bollard to boat.

Come out now and stand beside me,
look at the swans asleep,
tell me gossip about Keats,

drink your drink and smoke your cigarette,
let me ask you all those questions
or perhaps ask nothing.

The gulls say dawn is coming
but I believe that they are wrong
and the dark goes on for ever,

so come out now and stand here
in shirtsleeves although it's midwinter
quietly regarding water and stars.

The Inbox

It is the same electrical impulse as ever.
Look at the dates now: more than ten years
since that first empty message,

which was only your Hotmail address
blinking its way to my inbox
in slow, careful triumph

and with a touch of shyness: was this you, really,
using voice-recognition software
with such wary aplomb?

And then email after email went AWOL
and neither of us could work it out
until: *Yes, this time I got your brief note*

saying you had tried and tried, God knows
where the previous emails went
but now we're in business.

You tried to access the Kremlin webcam
to catch a glimpse of me there,
emailed my daughter to say how glad you were

that you did not have to learn Swedish
in order to enjoy Shakespeare.
Sometimes the software failed. *Lovelypage!*

you typed, *Didn't know of it before your email*
forgive brevity but my via-Voice is dumb.
I told you that crashing was all too common

and when the software worked, you wrote:
This celebrates the return
of your dictator father.

How far, how very far from that
you ever were.

Boatman

Give me that red tub like a child's drawing
give me the catamaran
or the ferry zig-zagging

give me any or all of them
and meanwhile hold tight to my hand
for the water is wide where we stand.

The water is wide where we stand
and we are weary with waiting
but the boatman will not come.

I gave you coins to hold ready
but it must have been then
that I looked away from the water

and the boat came and went
as you held on valiantly
with your small change for Charon.

We are cold and weary with waiting.
You say there is no boatman
there was never any boatman

and I say, hold tight to my hand
for the water is wide where we stand.

I Owned a Woman Once

so glossy-fleshed, so high-coloured
my blood swept in my veins
she was rich and heaped in the belly
as the Bible says
she was fertile as the bank of a river
when the flood falls and the mud makes food,

I clothed her as I wanted to clothe her
I housed her as I wanted to house her
I put food on her plate to fatten her,

I owned a woman once so high-coloured
so dark and rich in the eyes
my blood would not be still in my veins
my eyes would not stop watching her –
a callous on her heel made my belly quiver –

I put food on her plate to fatten her
I put oil on her hair
she was fertile as the bank of a river,

I owned a woman once so high-coloured
so slow and sure in her walk
that all eyes walked with her,
I owned her from broken toenail
to breath that misted my mirror

and I clothed her as I wanted to clothe her,
her flesh hidden, her body shrouded
while she fattened with my child,

yes, mostly it was sweet to own her
but sometimes I had to punish her
for her eyes everywhere looking
for all the moist folds of her body hidden
and the rich darkness of her eyes looking.

Soon it came to her time
and this woman I owed lay on the ground
in the room I kept for her
with the midwife I paid for her
but her belly would not release the child

and the cage of her hips would not let go the child.
The midwife said she came to it too young
maybe, this woman I owned

but believe me
she was straight out of the Bible
so glossy-fleshed, so high-coloured
so heaped and rich in the belly
with one bare callous on her heel.

When I should be working
on one of those afternoons
where the lights come on early
and rain spatters the windows
I take down an anthology
with a design of blue snowflakes
over the purple ground –
Longman English Series, Poetry
1900 to 1965
published (cased) in 1967.

T.S. Eliot looks desperate
in front of a BBC microphone
the size of a parking meter
and Thom Gunn's as glamorous
as his own sad captains.
In the margins, my husband's
young unreadable handwriting –
out of it springs a line,
a pulse of thought
he had years before we met.

In *Notes*, Lawrence is mildly taken to task
for the way his repetitions can degenerate,
though warmly praised for 'Gentians'.
I remember the teacher's voice
as we dug our heels into the flanks
of *Sons and Lovers*, on the home straight
or so we thought,
Does anyone know what he's on about?
Helen? But in Longman's Elysian
field the poems only answer
and the poets only ask.

Writ in Water

They make him a plaster saint of poetry, with his eyes turned up to heaven. But it wasn't like that.

Winter. Rome at last. The terrible voyage from England was done. We'd found lodgings and a doctor. All he had to do was to get well.

By day the noise of the fountain was almost hidden. There were women selling chickens and fresh milk, children playing, pails clattering, the creak of wheels and the clop of horses' hooves. We used to count the different sounds, and he always won. But at night the fountain played clearly. Bernini's fountain, with its fantastic coils of marble and gushing water.

'Our Roman water is pure, not like the filthy water in Napoli,' said our landlady, with a toss of her head. Signora Angeletti was slippery with the truth, but she was right about the water. I made sure there was always a full pitcher by his bed. Fever made him thirsty.

They've burned everything in our lodgings. The table we ate off, the bed he lay in. Even the shutters that I swung open at dawn so that he could gaze down the steps to the piazza and the life of a new day. They stripped our rooms. It's the law here. The Roman authorities are terrified of consumption.

'Please move aside, Signor Severn. We have our duty to perform.'

But the ceiling remains, the one he lay under. They couldn't take away those flowers he gazed at every day until he died. Sometimes he thought he was already in his grave, with flowers growing over him. He dreamed of water bubbling out of the earth, and violets in damp, sweet grass.

'You should be painting, Severn. Why are you not painting?'

When we first came, when he was strong enough, he would sit in the winter sun and watch the artists in the piazza.

'You have more talent than any of them, Severn.'

I still have this little sketch of him: see. There were others but they've been lost. Maybe someone has taken them, I don't know.

When you draw something, you never forget it. It was night, and there was one candle burning. That was enough light to draw by. It was a still, mild night, even though it was only February. But Spring comes early in Rome. It was the last night of his life.

The flame of the candle barely moved. The fountain was loud.

He was asleep, cast up on the pillow like a shipwrecked man. His hair was stuck to his forehead with sweat.

I shall never forget that night. He'd tried to prepare me. Warn me.

'Have you ever seen anyone die, Severn? I have. I nursed my brother Tom.'

Sometimes, after a fit of coughing, he would lie so still that I thought he was already dead.

'I must warn you, Severn, if you persist in nursing me you'll see nothing of Rome but a sickbed and a sick man. Believe me, it's better to give me the laudanum.'

There was a full bottle of laudanum. I gave it to him drop by drop, as Doctor Clarke ordered.

'Give me all of it, Severn. You don't understand what it is to die as I am going to die.'

But how could I allow him to destroy his immortal soul? I did not trust myself. I gave the laudanum to Dr Clarke, for fear I'd weaken.

He asked me to go the cemetery. He wanted me to describe the place where he was to lie. I told him about the goats cropping the grass, the young shepherd guarding his flock, the daisies and violets that grew so thickly over the graves.

'It's very quiet,' I told him. 'You can hear the breeze blowing through the grass. There's a pyramid which marks an ancient tomb.'

He lay back and closed his eyes. After a while he asked me whose tomb it was.

'I enquired,' I told him. 'His name was Caius Cestius, and he was a great man of the first century.'

'A great man... A very rich man at least, my dear Severn, if he had a pyramid built for his tomb. Is it large?'

'Large enough.'

'Does it cast a shadow?'

'I suppose so.'

His cough caught at him. I propped him with pillows.

'You should not talk,' I told him. He moved his head from side to side, restlessly. Then he said,

'You must understand that I will not regain my health now, Severn. I have studied enough anatomy to know that.'

We lived in our own world all those weeks. The next cup of broth, the next visit from Dr Clarke, the beating-up of pillows, the lighting of fires and measuring of medicines. Some days I hadn't a moment to call my own. Some nights I did not undress.

I was glad of it. He lay with the marble egg given to him by Miss Brawne in his hand. Women keep such an egg by them when they sew, to cool their fingers. He held that marble hour after hour, day after day. It soothed him as nothing else did. He wanted to know why he was still living, when everything was finished for him. This posthumous life, he called it.

He was sorry after he said it.

'My poor Severn, you have enough to do without listening to my misery.'

We had a piano carried upstairs so that I could play for him. He loved Haydn.

'Don't you hear that they are the same, Severn: the piano, and the fountain? Listen. But what am I thinking of? You cannot listen to yourself play, any more than a blackbird can hear itself sing.'

I was there as the days wore him down. His other friends, Dilke and Brown and Reynolds and the rest, they were far away in England. Now we fight over his memory like cats. But it was to me that he spoke. I wiped the sweat off his face and washed him and changed his linen. I told him about the sheep that roamed over the graves. He smiled. He never tired of the sheep, the goats, the shepherd boy and the violets. The next day he would ask again, as if he'd already forgotten.

But I don't think he forgot. Words were like notes of music to him. He liked to hear how they fell.

'Sometimes I think I am already buried, with flowers growing over me,' he said, as he stared up at the ceiling where the painted flowers swarmed.

Signora Angeletti became suspicious. She waylaid the doctor, asking what was wrong. Was it consumption?

'I am a charitable woman, but I must think of my other lodgers.'

I didn't know the laws of Rome then. She feared that they would strip her rooms and burn everything. I suppose she was right, but she was compensated. She lost nothing.

I heard the patter of Signora Angeletti's voice from the mezzanine. We were in her hands. No other boarding-house would take us now: he was too obviously ill.

He understood Signora Angeletti very well. She gave us a bad dinner, not long after we came, and he threw it straight out of the window onto the Steps. A crowd of urchins came from nowhere and scrabbled for it.

'She won't serve us such stuff again,' he said, and he was right. She had given us rubbish, to see if we were willing to swallow it. I wished I had his firmness. I was nervous with Signora Angeletti, and she knew it. In those ways he was more worldly than I was.

Yes, they make him a plaster saint of poetry, with his eyes turned up to heaven. They fight over his memory, shaping it this way and that. But I remember how he rocked with laughter when that dinner splattered on the marble steps!

'My best plate!' screamed Signora Angeletti. But he said,

'If that plate is the best you have, Signora, then I am very sorry for you.'

After that the dinners were always hot and good.

I've told the story of those months so many times that they hardly seem to belong to me. If I say that they were the high point of my life, you will misunderstand me. You may even accuse me of cruelty. A man lay dying, and I say it was the high point of my existence? How can I recall those months of agony and dwindling hope, except with a shudder?

I remember the nights chiefly. We set the candles so that as one died, the next one would light from its burning thread. Once he said that there was a fairy lamplighter in the room. The flame would burn down until it seemed about to collapse on itself. He watched intently all the while. When the next sprang up and began to bloom, he would allow himself to close his eyes.

When I was very tired the room seemed to sway and the noise of the fountain reminded me of our voyage from England. Sometimes I fell asleep for a few seconds and really believed that I felt the motion of the ship under me.

I remember one incident which I have never written down, or spoken of even. I was in the small room which was intended for my studio. I thought of his words.

'You should be painting, Severn! Here you are in Rome and you do not paint at all.'

I was standing at the table, going through my sketchbook. It contained a few studies which I hoped might be worth further work. I had sketched the cemetery for him. The pyramid of Caius Cestius, with the young shepherd sitting on the grass. But I had never shown him the sketch. How can a man say to another:

'Look, here is the place where you will be buried. Just there, where that shepherd sits and dreams.'

I decided to be buried there too, beside him. My heart grew

easier then. I felt no more estrangement from him.

As I turned the pages of my sketchbook, a cruel truth hit me like a blow. The reason I could not paint was not so much my cares for the invalid, as my fear that I would never paint well enough. Here I was in Rome, the heart of the painted world. Here were my masters all around me. Nothing I achieved could ever equal one of Bernini's marble coils.

The noise of the fountain grew louder. It was drowning me. It told to give up, stop pretending that there was merit in my pitiful daubs or in the travelling scholarship I'd been so proud to win. Rome would wash me away, as it had washed away a thousand others, leaving no trace. I seized hold of the leaves of my sketchbook, meaning to rip them out so that no one would ever guess the contemptible folly of my ambitions.

At that moment I felt a touch on my shoulder. A clasp, a warm, wordless, brotherly clasp. The fingers gripped my shoulder and then shook it a little, consolingly, encouragingly.

I knew straightaway that it was him. God knows how he had dragged himself out of that bed and come to find me. I could not imagine how he'd guessed at my anguish. I said nothing. His clasp was enough. After a moment the grip of the hand tightened, and then left me.

He was going back to bed, I thought. But there were no retreating footsteps. I looked over my shoulder. No one was there. He could not possibly have moved so fast. I hurried to the bedroom and there he was, deeply asleep. I stared at his face and I knew that he was dying, not weeks or months in the future, but now. How had I not recognised it before?

I sat down by the bed. My sketchbook was still in my hand. I got up again, noiselessly, and fetched what I needed from the little room. I was ready to draw him now.

The noise of the fountain. The sound of a pencil moving. His breath. A long, dragging pause. Another breath. You can live an entire life between one breath and the next. That's where my life was spent, in one night, in one room. The rest is memory.

Dis

The obvious story, my darling,
is that Dis caught you
into his dark kingdom.

I don't know where I was
when he seared the grass
with winter footprints.

If your mother was not there
whose hand could hold you
when he opened the earth for you?

I see your fingers
twist in your lap
as you keep mute.

You will not eat the seeds.
You know what he offers you.
They glow softly, like coral

in the blue vaults of this hell
where I am only a shadow
squeaking its anguish.

Let me take your place in the dark.
Dis knows you have eaten nothing
of his gifts, his pomegranates.

For months he's kept you,
whispering 'Your mother
never loved you as I love you.'

Part your hands, my darling.
Let me pour into them
salt and grain.

Newgate

Beneath the bulk of the block the bins
sweat with a week's refuse.
In the concrete corridor lines of lockers
gape, hiding a man who's

back-to-the-wall, intent
as the last words of his sentence
lock together, his own jigsaw
starting to make sense.

He tunes up a stifle of terror
in the girl he's got by the throat
while she claws at his fingers.
He's bored. He flicks the remote.

He's had enough of all this noise
and endless interference –
lights going out, pupils pinpoints.
Why can't they let him be as he is?

Far away a bin lid drops down
and the arches of Newgate tighten
as dead men walk through them
on the way to their dying.

What architect first squinnied
to fix this perspective? Getting it right
meant waiting for the reaction
when it came into sight.

Now they are breathing. Now
guards shovel the quicklime.
Now the girl uncurls from her sofa,
and takes the rubbish down.

The guards whistle, nonchalant
as the prison van backs up.
Even now the soiled dark of the cell
even now the thrash of the girl.

At Ease

When I was four at the feet
of my grandpa and my great-uncle
we heard how well Frank had done

all those years with his war pension.
He got the better of them.
They doled it when he was young

mustard-gassed and not likely to live
long enough to do more than dint it –
but he married on it.

That was in the Great War
when my grandpa kept order
in the burning Dardanelles.

You wouldn't guess how many flowers
grew in those brown hills.
For a month they bled anemones

then they were blue with hyacinths –
little wild ones, not like these.

Harbinger

Small, polished shield-bearer
abacus of early days
and harbinger of life's happiness

that the world offers
things scarlet and spotted
to alight, hasping and unhasping
unlikely wings,

that there can be three or thousands
but not a plague of ladybirds
no, a benediction of ladybirds
to enamel the weeds.

Small, polished shield-bearer
abacus of early days,
harbinger of life's happiness.

The Hyacinths

Pressed in the soil's black web, nursed by the rough
offhand embrace of frost, the hyacinths
turn in their sleep. Such blunt stabbings
against the paperiness of ancient skin,
such cell-memory, igniting
a slow fuse laid in the ground.

Pressed in the soil's black web, rocked back to sleep
by the storm that tugs at the holly tree's roots
the hyacinths know they are listening
to the west wind that kills them,
but they are safe, having given themselves to darkness.
All they desire is not to flower.

Hyacinths, when I see you forced from the soil
glossy and over-talkative
with your loud scent and demand for attention
I will put you back to sleep, forking
the long-fibred darkness over you.

The Night Workers

All you who are awake in the dark of the night,
all you companions of the one lit window
in the knuckled-down row of sleeping houses,

all you who think nothing of the midnight hour
but by three or four have done your work
and are on the way home, stopping

at traffic lights, even though there is no one
but you in either direction. How different the dark is
when day is coming; you know all this.

All you who have kept awake through the dark of the night
and now go homeward; you, charged with the hospital's
vending-machine coffee; you working all night at Tesco,

you cleaners and night-club toilet attendants,
all you wearily waiting for buses
driven by more of you, men who paint lines

in the quiet of night, women with babies
roused out of their sleep so often
they've given up and stand by their windows

watching the fog of pure neon
weaken at the rainy dawn's coming.

Agapanthus above Porthmeor

(for Patrick and Alexa)

Blue against blue; blue into deeper blue.
Skeins of light at the horizon
and the flower here, touchable,
a blue that gathers to it
the sky, the sea.

Tender, exotic,
the agapanthus was not born here
but it belongs here
with its own essence of blue
echoing the sea's deep stripes.

You pause on the hill, breathless
and look back at the silk of the horizon
at the wide miles you have climbed
to be together, here
and wanting nothing.

Blue against blue, blue into deeper blue.
This is the day of the agapanthus,
of flower-filled sureness.
Love is here, touchable,
gathering our lives to it.

Visible and Invisible

(for Jane)

That dream when we were young,
that hunt for the magic
which might make it happen:
invisibility.

Such glittering cloaks
such eagerly swallowed
rose-petal potions

but we stayed solid and sunlit
jumping on our own shadows
defeated by ourselves.

We didn't know how easy
the trick would turn out to be.
All you do is let the years pass

and quietly on its own it happens.
You only have to let the airy cloak of years
fall on your shoulders.

The Snowfield

No matter how wide the snowfield
you don't walk in your own footprints –
each day the apparent freedom
narrows, sun greases
your steps to ice

until the steep track glistens beneath you
and you dare not go on
but stand trembling
bruised, struggling to balance,

you stand trembling as night comes on
on the wicked lip of the hill that stands
between you and home.

Lemon tree in November
(for Kurt and Caroline Jackson)

Dark, present, scattering night,
the blows of the wind
on the upturned hull of home

the stub of the lighthouse wiped out
the land crouched

our lemon tree
shaking its leaves
in the wet garden

the palm at the window
hissing, rattling

as the lighthouse beam
buds and grows
on a gnarl of foam.

Dark, present, scattering night
with the curtains bulging
and the wind again
on the upturned hull of home.

Bildad

The dark, present, scattering night,
the thick stub of the light-house folded
and put away like linen
but still the bud of its light opening
over a gnarl of foam,

such an oncoming
dark in the garden
the slim leaves of the lemon tree
quite gone,
its structure hung
by the light of its fruit.

Palm leaves hiss
in the rough hands of the wind,
that wind again
kneading the air as it wants –
The more the decades
the less we belong,
tangential as thistle
while the wind booms

seizing the chimneys
lifting the curl
of our ill-made sunroof.
Untouchable
the wind does what it wants
playing harmonica
on the upturned hull of home:

such quaintness
to build a house here,
to slip a bribe to the rock
not to open under it
and pay the sea to turn back.

Tonight the ravaging of cliffs
is the hunger of pack-animals
jostling for place,
hunting the man named Job
in the land of Uz

whose imagination painted him
a righteous kingdom
where he washed his steps with butter.
But the wind answered him
and *naked*, Job said, *I came
and naked will return*
as he sat on the ground.

The wind scours our faces with stars.
We wriggle like children
eyes screwed up tight,
our quaint imaginations
busy planting lemons
lulled by the ear-drowse
and zing of bees.

There is a cup, blue, full to the brim
with tea. There is catnip
and the brief shade of an olive tree.
Outside, a dusty road, and from time to time
walkers, who greet each other with silence
or a curt nod which affirms
the rubric of the stranger
and we are all strangers here.

At the far side of the earth's curve
waiting to flood our habitations
there is always the night
borne on a wind beyond imagination
and not to be troubled with,
a wind that chases its load of stars
like dust beneath the broom,

There is the dark, present, scattering night,
the thick stub of the light-house folded
and put away like linen,
the bud of its light blocked
by the bulk of a new roof.

Bildad said: *how can he be clean*
that is born of a woman?
And so answers a mob of men
hunting down a girl
with a wind of sticks and stones
as they strip her and beat her
from town to town
assisted by bicycles
and mobile phones.

I trouble myself with the snipping of catnip.
If I sit on the ground
it will comfort no one
and rake no spittle from the wind.

Skulking

A heap of cloud
skulks over the roofs
like the summit of a bully's ambition –

the short dark days of winter
dear to me
as a bully to his mother.

Basement at Eighteen Folgate Street

I know them by their shoes –
clean kid on a Sunday,
work-boots on Mondays
chipping sparks from the pavement,
or skittery dance shoes
going to the Palais on a Saturday –
the cuff-cuff-cuff of too many lives –

Barclays Bank, St Ives

Old men with sticks and courteous greeting
who have learned the goodness of days
and give freely the hours it takes
to reach the fathomless depth of the pipe's tamped bowl
or the corolla of that daffodil
damply unfolding, or a toothless smile from a pushchair
that irradiates the granite morning.

One of them puts out a finger
dark with work and nicotine
to touch the blooming cheek of a great-granddaughter.
How close they are to the rim of the earth
while the cashpoint zizzes out figures
and the young go up and down the street with backpacks,
their eyes justified and full of purpose.

Playing Her Pieces
(for Thomas Hardy in 1912)

He takes the temperature of his heart.
O feverish instrument that played so crazily
with such wild fingers and still struck
dead on the note,

is it cool yet? Does it stand apart
like a man civilly bowing a woman
whom he no longer loves
through a door he will not enter?

O feverish instrument of art,
he kneels beside the body of his love
to wash his hands between her ribs
where the blood throbbed.

Look at her playing her pieces. Start
her song again, the one that wearied him
as her dull flesh wearied him, her stiff
intransigent difficultness –

all of it laved now. Let his fingers part
as her soul slips through them –
O feverish instrument, let
the man sit and write.

Pianist, 103,

looks at the morning
where she will play
from nine to one
and says how beautiful
each note, each sun.

Such scales of suffering –
no one can weigh them,
she says how beautiful
each smile, each footfall
each startled face
in the heat of love –

The Torn Ship

In what torn ship soever I embark
That ship shall be my emblem of Thy ark...

JOHN DONNE,
'A Hymn to Christ, at the Author's Last Going into Germany'

I was up and watching
that night the torn ship rode
through the lock gates and so came on –

In the guise of midnight
it slowly glided
owl-like in stubborn purpose
broken by the hands of the storm.

So it came on
blackly on the black water,
pulse by pulse it found harbour –
Through the shut lock gates it melted

to the ring and rocking
of a hundred tall masts
and then the swans woke from their nest
and stood unfurling

their steeple wings in warning
as the shade and shadow passed
of whatsoever torn ship it was.
Remember this was no ark

but something broken
long before the dark took it down.

Taken in Shadows

Beautiful John Donne. Who wouldn't want you? You lean slightly forward, arms folded over your body as if to protect it from all the women who might otherwise tear off your clothes.

And yet, now that I look closely – and I do look very, very closely, John – there's a teasing touch of something I can only call ...*readiness*...in the way you're sitting for your portrait. Take your eyes. They are clear hazel, brooding on something that is beyond me and a little to my right. What has caught your gaze? How many generations of women – and men too, I'm sure, men too – must have longed to make you turn to them. But your gaze has never shifted. Not once, in over four centuries.

Your mouth is red. The shadow of your moustache – so dandyish, so eloquently shaved into points! – serves to emphasise the perfect cut of your upper lip. Your lower lip is full, sensuous. Red lips, hazel eyes, arched, dark eyebrows. Your jaw is a line of perfection. The shadow of your broad-brimmed hat can't hide the modelling of your temples. Your long fingers rest on your sleeve's rich satin. You gleam in light from a source which is forever invisible, outside the frame. And then there's the fall of your collar, the exquisiteness of lace thrown over darkness.

You're in your glory. From where you sit inside your portrait, it's the present day. The present moment, even, and you're caught in it. Your right ankle itches, but you suppress the urge to scratch. Your heart throbs with its own quick life. Soon the sitting will be over, but you don't mind the time you spend here. The artist is anonymous to me, but not to you. You know him well. This portrait is important to you and you'll keep it with you all your life.

The moment I look away, you smile, stand up and stretch like a cat. The artist, of course, has taken careful note of your pose before it dissolves.

'Until next time,' he says, wiping a brush.

'Until next time,' you agree.

You've given me the slip again, John. You're back in your own world. It's 1595, a date which I know well. I've studied your period, and I dress you in my rags of knowledge. I can analyse your social status in the light of your lace collar. You are history, John. You wouldn't like that, I know. The fact that I can speak and you cannot would seem quite wrong to you, given the relative values of what we have to say.

You know 1595 from the inside, by the touch of satin, the warmth of a spring day, the gamey smell of your own body, the bite of a flea at the nape of your neck. For you, the door is about to open into a stream of May sunshine that will make you blink. For me, it has closed forever.

The Elizabethan age has eight more years to run. The old Queen has kept the show on the road so much longer and more brilliantly than anyone had a right to expect. She has united the country. Those who are not united are dead, imprisoned, exiled, silenced or lying very low indeed.

You're in your glory, but also in those shadows that wrap themselves around you like a cloak. Your mother has gone into exile, and your brother died in Newgate two years ago, because he harboured a priest. Your fellow Catholics are food for the scaffold. That is what hanging, drawing and quartering is all about. It does so much more than kill: it turns a protesting soul into blood-slimed joints of meat, laid on the block for the public appetite.

You don't yet know for sure that England will not return to the faith, not soon, not ever, but I should say that you've already made an educated guess. You have, as we know, a great deal of imagination. You will do nothing which will allow your body to be seized, racked, beaten, imprisoned, to die in its own shit and blood and vomit on the clammy ground. You will not be carted to Tyburn to be pelted with the crowd's insults, spittle and rotten fruit before you are lynched. Nor are you willing to endure the long, dismal martyrdom of being jobless, without influence, friends or position, bled dry by penal taxes. You are already preparing to leave the home of your soul, and find another if you can.

I look at your long, slender fingers. Perhaps you played upon the lute, as well as upon the emotions of a hundred women. Beautiful, beautiful John Donne. How were you to know that there'd be generations snuffling greedily over your portrait? You couldn't guess, any more than Sylvia Plath guessed what would happen to her image after the lens clicked, her radiant smile faded and she got up from where she'd been sitting on a bank of daffodils with her infant son in her arms. How could you estimate the wolfish hunger of a public not yet born?

You and Sylvia are the kind we really love. You make us feel that we can climb right inside your lives. The only frustrating thing is that you keep looking at things we cannot see. You will never meet our eyes.

Listen, John, I can tell you what's going to happen to you after you take off that lace collar. You're going to screw up on a royal scale. You'll fall in love with the wrong girl, miscalculate about her father coming round to your secret marriage (he won't, not for years). You'll find yourself in a cottage full of children, most of whom have coughs or colds or sweating sickness or some other early seventeenth-century malady, for much of the time. Life will become an everlasting winter, smelling of herbs, baby shit, sour milk and dirty clothes.

John Donne
Anne Donne
Undone

I wonder what your wife thought when she read that little epigram? Some of your children will die, or be born dead. With any luck you won't feel it as we would these days. Poor little rabbits, you'll be sorry enough for them while they're alive, screaming their heads off, wanting all the things that nobody's able to give them, such as antibiotics, central heating and a trip to Disneyland.

I expect your wife will have to sell that lace collar to pay for one of her confinements. You'll lose your job. Everyone who owes you a grudge will take the chance to kick you now that you're down. You'll be out of favour for years. For all the effort you've put into avoiding martyrdom, you'll achieve your own not very glorious exile in a borrowed cottage in Mitcham.

But none of that has happened yet.

'Come and look,' says the artist, and you saunter round to his side of the easel. Next week he will begin to paint your hands. It has already been decided that you will wear no rings. You don't need to trumpet your status or your prospects, and besides, the artist prefers not to mar the effect of your long, eloquent fingers.

You stare thoughtfully at your unfinished portrait. It will wreak havoc for generations, that painted face. Cohorts of fifteen-year-old girls will fall for you and feel for you, as you struggle in the swamp of domesticity. *'His wife had a baby a year, isn't that gross? She must of been pregnant, like, all the time.'*

But your true lovers are more sensitive. We know the inside

story. You were undone indeed, you and Anne. A piece of her soul went awry when she married you, and a piece of your soul left your body to meet it. You were never intact again. You tried to write with the noise of your little ones ringing in your ears. You went upstairs, you went downstairs, you went up to town and down to the country, you went to my lady's chamber but there they still were, babbling, squabbling, screaming and squawking, catching quinsies and spotted fevers and scarlet fevers and marsh fevers.

You had no money and each child cost so much. Months of sickness and weariness for Anne, heavy clambering of the stairs, dull aches that heralded the rack of labour. The children's voices floated, skirling. Tom fought with John, Constance bossed little Mary.

Mary died. Baby Nicholas died. The stillborn unnamed baby died. They floated off, little eager vagrant souls who had found flesh, but not for quite long enough. They were turned out of their bodies like tenants who hadn't paid the rent. They left fragments of themselves: their blind, eager sucking, the drum of their feet inside the womb. Mary's first words drifted around your house like feathers.

I was one of those fifteen-year-olds, of course, and head-over-heels in love with you. You were so unhappy. With what brave grace you wrote of your 'hospital at Mitcham' where the children grew and the poems shrank. You were kept busy writing begging letters. You had to have patrons, even though so many had turned their backs. No one wants to be contaminated by social failure. You'd stepped out so boldly and now you had to fight for a foothold somewhere, anywhere.

I would have done anything for you, when I was fifteen. I even made friends with your wife. Yes, in that hasty, obsequious way of a very determined girl when she pits herself against a grown woman and a mother. I could babysit for Anne perhaps. Surely she would like to have a nice sit down? I shepherded little Constance and John and Tom and Mary into the other room, sang sweetly to them, gave them their dinner and washed their bare, rosy feet. A curl of green snot crawled in and out of Mary's nostril as she breathed. I found a rag and wiped it away tenderly.

There was silence from the bedroom. Anne must be sleeping, I thought, and no wonder. Her pregnancy looked like a growth on her skinny body. Her skin was blue-white. She wore a married woman's cap and the hair that escaped from it was thin and lustreless.

I wonder, by my troth, what thou and I
Did til we loved?

Let Anne sleep for a while, poor thing. I didn't want the children to wake her, so I hoisted Mary onto my knee and began to tell a story. She twisted round in my lap and pressed my lips together with her fingers. The others pinched and poked and whinged. I couldn't even come up with a nursery rhyme. It was time to wake Anne up again.

I tiptoed to the door of her bedroom. Your bedroom too, but I prefer not to think about that. I heard something I didn't expect: laughter. A slash of dread went through me. You'd got in there somehow. You were laughing with her, privately. But no. I peeped through the gap in the door and there she was, quite alone, sitting up in bed and reading. A few seconds later she laughed again, and looked up with vague shining eyes as if she expected someone. She didn't see me, of course.

I've put a stop to all that sort of thing. I'm not fifteen any more. The past is the past and it's better, much better for everyone, if it doesn't come alive. I don't want to see your beautiful face grow old. I don't want to see your wife's plain, worn features light up when she thinks I might be you, ready to share her laughter. I went too far that time, but I've pulled myself back and I'm in command again. You are history, John. You've written all your poems. Your tongue is still. I refuse to be coerced into seeing things your way.

You're back inside the portrait frame, beautiful and contained. Your red lips. Your high cheekbones and the pure almond cut of your eyelids. It's no surprise that you liked this portrait so much. What a blend of sexual magnetism and intellectual glamour. But I've just noticed something else that I've never seen before. There's a glint of humour in your eyes, as if you're wondering how many more centuries of devastation you'll be capable of before your painted magic fades. There are just the two of us, John. Why won't you look at me? Why won't you tell me what you see?

Prince Felipe Prospero

(1657-1661)

He wears a silver bell
so that in the shadow
of palace corridors
he can always be followed,

he wears a ball of amber
to ward off infection,
he wears an amulet
against malediction,

so blessed and protected
with hair like thistledown
and a gaze the painter
'found in heaven'.

He wears the slightest of frowns
but keeps to his station
as we do, watching him.

Picture Messages

of trees: olive and lemon,
of eggs and bacon
of my father at The Tin Drum
on his last weekend
smiling,
with coffee in front of him.

We went to Latinos
to eat *gambas a la plancha*
while you chatted to Mariella,
we went home and you sat
in the red armchair.
Your hand took mine:
it was that half hour before departing.

You took my bag to the door
and had your hand on the lift button
as usual pretending surprise
that anyone could shun
the judder of that contraption
with its random halts between floors,

I said I would see you soon
after a last embrace,
and you kept your hand raised
until I was swallowed
in the dark of the turning staircase.

Lethe

Is it Lethe or is it dock water?
Either has the power.

The neighbourhood killer
is somewhere quietly washing up

dipping and dipping his fork
in the dirty water.

The police vans sit crooning
on the crux of the Downs.

How quickly the young girls walk
from work and from the shops.

The frost that was bone cold
has eased into rain, the dock water

takes everything and turns it brown.

The Queue's Essentially

The queue's essentially
docile surges get us
very slowly somewhere.

Like campfire, life springs up –
that pair ahead of me
(newly landed on Easyjet, he
shunts the wheeled, packed
tartan suitcase
inch by inch

through jumpy fractures of brake-light
on wet pavement) –

that pair ahead of me
who graze on their vegetable pasty
and pass it in Polish
from his hand to hers –

so intimate, rained-upon –
learning so quickly it will be a mistake
to take that taxi
all the way to Kilburn –

The Captainess of Laundry

I am the captainess of laundry
and I sing to its brave tune,
to the crack and the whip and the flap of the sheets
and the rack going up, going down, going down
and the rack going up and going down,

I am the captainess of laundry
and I salt my speech with a song
of the bleach and the blue and the colours holding true
and the glaze of the starch on my skin, my skin,
and the glaze of starch on my skin,

I am the captainess of laundry
and I swing my basket through the town
with the sheets and the shirts and the white petticoats
and a snowy-breasted cover tied around, tied around
and a snowy-breasted cover tied around.

The Day's Umbrellas

On the same posts each evening
the harbour cormorants
hang out their wings to dry
like the day's umbrellas
as the late ferry passes.

In sour-sweet ramparts of ivy
the blackbirds call
drowsily, piercingly.
Above them the gulls
are casing the terraces.

Thickly, the pigeons
groom their own voices
as parents in the half-light
tiptoe away from babies
over their heads in sleep.

The Deciphering

How busy we are with the dead in their infancy,
who are still damp with the sweat of their passing,
whose hair falls back to reveal a scar.

We think of wiping their skin, attending them
in the old way, but are timid, ignorant.
We walk from the high table where they are laid

leaving their flesh royally mounded
just as they have left it
for the undertakers to cherish.

We consider the last kiss,
the taste and the grain of it.
The lift doors squeeze open, then shut.

All day we think that we have lost our car keys.
There is a feeling in the back of the mind
as we eat a meal out on the balcony

but the door refuses to open
and although my sisters have prepared food elaborately
you do not advance to us, smiling.

The children have put sauce on the side of their plates
thinking you will come and swipe a chip,
thinking this meal is one you cooked

as always, humming to yourself in the kitchen,
breaking off to tap the barometer
and watch starlings roost on the pier.

How long it takes to stop being busy with that day,
each second of it like the shard
of a pot which someone has laboured to dig up

and piece together without knowledge
of language or context.
Slow, slow, the deciphering.

The Tarn

Still as the water is
the wind draws on it in iron

this is the purple country, the border
where we threw ourselves down
onto the heather.

Even the lapwing knows how to pretend.
She runs with her broken wing
to hide the fact of her young.

A cold small rain spatters the tarn
the wind writes on the dark water.

The Gift

You never wanted the taste
of the future on your tongue.
How often, hurriedly, I saw you
swallow a premonition.

If the gift comes, you told me,
do not let it in.
Obedient, I wrote poems
but the gift still came

though the doors were bolted.
I'm here, it told me
*to make you know things
but not their names.*

What Will You Say

(after Baudelaire)

What will you say, my soul, poor and alone,
and my heart with its heart sucked out,
What will you say tonight to *the one*
(if she's really the one this time)?

totheverybeautifultotheverygoodtotheverydear
Ah no. Speak clearly. What will you say
to her, so good, so fair, so dear
whose heavenly gaze has made your desert flower?

You'll say you've had enough. No more.
You've no pride left but what goes to praise her.
No strength left but in her douce power,
no senses but what she gives.

Sweet authority! Douce power!
or do you mean you're shit-scared
to go anywhere without her?
Is she your mother?

Her look clothes us in light.
Her ghost is the scent of a rose.
Let her ghost dance with the air
let its torch blaze through the streets –

You'd like that, no doubt.
When you've given up running after her
her ghost will issue commands
to do what you've already done.

It's over with you. If she won't feed you
you must stay hungry. She is your guardian
angel, your bodyguard, no one
comes close, you can't love anyone.

Cloud

Nature came to us abhorring sharp edges
raw sunlight and the absence of cloud:

it is November deep in the mist
and by a gate a man stands lost in thought –

how that farm hunkers ruddily in a crease of land
and the dog yaps into the twilight –

We used to say we were walking in the cloud
do you remember? – and we were born there

natives of chrysanthemums, bonfire afternoons,
makers of the finest shades of meaning.

Low over the hill the cloud hangs.
Mist fills the serrations of plough.

I Have Been Thinking of You So Loudly

I have been thinking of you so loudly
that perhaps as you walked down the street you turned
on hearing your name's decibels
sing from pavement, hoardings and walls

until like glass from last night's disasters
your name shattered. Soon sweepers will come
and all my love of you will vanish
as if it had never been.

Meanwhile, hurry before lateness catches you,
run until the wind blows out your coat,
don't stand irresolute
like me, thinking too loudly.

The Kingdom of the Dead

The kingdom of the dead is like an owl
in the heart of the city, hunting
at the Downs' margin.
Over Carter's Steam Fair,
over the illicitly parked cars
where lovers tighten and quicken,
it glides with a tilt of the wing.

The kingdom of the dead is like a mouse
in the owl's eye, a streak of brown
at the Downs' margin.
Under the bright hooves of Carter's horses it hides
this mouse, a drop of water
which flows in its terror
into a beer can.

The kingdom of the dead is like the boot
of a boy in the bliss of fair-time
rucking the grass at the Downs' margin.
Carter's is turning out now, he runs
in and out of the horses
and kicks the beer can
into the touch of heaven.

The Last Heartbeat

The last heartbeat washes the body clean of pain
in a tide of endorphins,
the last sound coils into the ears, and stirs
ossicles, cochlea, the tiny hairs.

For a day or more
long after the onlookers
have turned away
thinking it's all over

the firework show of synapses
and the glorious near-touch
of axons in the brain
slowly dies down
to a last, exquisite connection.

The Old Mastery

Weary and longing to go home
you dress slowly.
Not much of your wardrobe likes you.

You reach for those trousers again
and buff up your shoes
with the old mastery.

The Overcoat

It wears a smell of earth, not air.
I am under it forever.
Sometimes I sleep, sometimes I shiver.

There is a map and I am on it.
the bed's icy geography
is iron, dust-devil, ticking.

Sometimes I fetch from my dreams
the shapes of neighbours, friends,
the smell of rubber perishing.

Sometimes the bed-springs groan
under the weight of the coat.
It will not let me out.

I hold fear so steadily
it stays all in one piece.
I hold the coat's collar.

I hold my breath while the ghost
that lives inside it slides past me
and is bequeathed.

Window Cleaners at Ladysmith Road

Some swear by vinegar and some by newspaper.
Some brandish a shammy leather.

Here they come with their creamy forearms,
their raw red hands, pinnies and aprons
until they stand at my shoulder.

I smell them but don't dare turn.
They are judging smears on the glass,
and as for me and the present
they'll soon have that off.

A warped shine shows the street buckling
into the past, as helpless as I am
not to reflect those boys on the corner
smoking Woodbines from the tobacconist's
which no longer exists.

I Heard You Sing in the Dark
(for Tess)

I heard you sing in the dark
a few clear notes on the stairs

a blackbird in the cold of dusk
forever folding your wings

and slipping, rustling down
past leaves and ivy knots

to where your song bubbled
out of the crevices
into cold, clear February dusk.

I heard the notes plain
rising to the surface
of evening and then down again

almost chuckling, in a blackbird's cold
liquid delight, and so I turned
on the landing, and you were gone.

La Recouvrance

The schooner *La Recouvrance* is almost at the horizon now, sailing south-west. Much closer, the sea is recovering ground. In town the equinoctial spring tides will bring water up the slipway, over the wall and into the sandbagged streets. But here the tide can rise as far as it likes. This cove will be swallowed up soon. Anyone foolish enough to wait too long before they climb the rocks will be washed away like their own footprints. Each small, collapsing wave darkens another arc of the white sand. If you watch it like this you'll be entranced and you won't move until it's too late. Today the sea has a particular smell that isn't like sea at all. If you had your eyes closed you would guess at flowers in the distance. Nothing sweet or perfumed, but a sharp, early narcissus.

You've brought the child down here with you, although it's not very safe. You lift her over the clefts and gullies, carrying everything you need in a backpack and coming back for her. She waits for you obediently, perched above the drop.

There are just the two of you in the sea. Thigh deep, and now waist deep. The incoming tide pushes against you, and you hold the child's hand, but there are no rips here. Every so often a wave lifts her off her feet. She can swim quite strongly now, and the lift of the sea makes her laugh, showing her sharp little teeth. She dips her head under a wave and brings it up. Her long hair is plastered to her skull and water streams down her face, shining.

You say it's time to go now. She swims into your arms and her strong, cold little body clings to yours. She winds her legs around your waist. Together you stagger towards the shore, but while you are still in the sea's embrace you turn back to see *La Recouvrance* *one* last time. Her tall masts have vanished. Already she has dipped below the horizon, as she sails away to the bottom of the world.

The Filament

Step by step, holding the thread,
step by step into the dark,

step by step, holding a flag of light
where the tunnel in secrecy closes
like fist or crocus.

My footsteps follow your footsteps
into the dark where they are still
after all these years
just beyond my hearing,

so I call to you in the language
that even now we speak
because you taught me to be haunted
by the catch and space of it –
because we paid for it.

At the tunnel's end a black lake,
a small, desultory boat,
the pluck of the water
as the boat shapes from the shore
while a boatman reads his newspaper
with a desultory air.

The cave roof glistens.
The ribs and flanks of the chamber
all give back the dark water.
I am ready for the journey –
Shall we take ship together? –

Shall we lift my torch into the boat
and sit athwart?
Shall we pass our hands quickly
through crocus and saffron

like children playing with matches?
Even if the boat never sets sail
we can be content,

and I won't look at your face
or write another word.

Glad of These Times

(2007)

For Maurice Dunmore

1928-2006

City lilacs

In crack-haunted alleys, overhangs,
plots of sour earth that pass for gardens,
in the space between wall and wheelie bin,

where men with mobiles make urgent conversation,
where bare-legged girls shiver in April winds,
where a new mother stands on her doorstep and blinks
at the brightness of morning, so suddenly born –

in all these places the city lilacs are pushing
their cones of blossom into the spring
to be taken by the warm wind.

Lilac, like love, makes no distinction.
It will open for anyone.
Even before love knows that it is love
lilac knows it must blossom.

In crack-haunted alleys, in overhangs,
in somebody's front garden
abandoned to crisp packets and cans,

on landscaped motorway roundabouts,
in the depth of parks
where men and women are lost in transactions
of flesh and cash, where mobiles ring

and the deal is done – here the city lilacs
release their sweet, wild perfume
then bow down, heavy with rain.

Crossing the field

To live your life is not as simple as to cross a field.

RUSSIAN PROVERB

To cross the field on a sunset of spider-webs
sprung and shining, thistle heads
white with tufts that are harvest
tended and brought to fruit by no one,

to cross the long field as the sun goes down
and the whale-back Scillies show damson
twenty miles off, as the wind sculls
out back, and five lighthouses
one by one open their eyes,

to cross the long field as it darkens
when rooks are homeward, and gulls
swing out from the tilt of land
to the breast of ocean – now is the time
the vixen stirs, and the green lane's
vivid with footprints.

A field is enough to spend a life in.
Harrow, granite and mattress springs,
shards and bones, turquoise droppings
from pigeons that gorge on nightshade berries,
a charm of goldfinch, a flight of linnets,
fieldfare and January redwing
venturing westward in the dusk,
all are folded in the dark of the field,

all are folded into the dark of the field
and need more days
to paint them, than life gives.

Litany

For the length of time it takes a bruise to fade
for the heavy weight on getting out of bed,
for the hair's grey, for the skin's tired grain,
for the spider naevus and drinker's nose
for the vocabulary of palliation and Macmillan
for friends who know the best funeral readings,

for the everydayness of pain, for waiting patiently
to ask the pharmacist about your medication
for elastic bandages and ulcer dressings,
for knowing what to say
when your friend says how much she still misses him,
for needing a coat although it is warm,

for the length of time it takes a wound to heal,
for the strange pity you feel
when told off by the blank sure faces
of the young who own and know everything,
for the bare flesh of the next generation,
for the word 'generation', which used to mean nothing.

Don't count John among the dreams

*(i.m. John Kipling, son of Rudyard Kipling,
who died in the Battle of Loos in 1915)*

Don't count John among the dreams
a parent cherishes for his children –
that they will be different from him,
not poets but the stuff of poems.

Don't count John among the dreams
of leaders, warriors, eagle-eyed stalkers
picking up the track of lions.
Even in the zoo he can barely see them –

his eyes, like yours, are half-blind.
Short, obedient, hirsute
how he would love to delight you.
He reads every word you write.

Don't count John among your dreams.
Don't wangle a commission for him,
don't wangle a death for him.
He is barely eighteen.

Without his spectacles, after a shell-blast,
he will be seen one more time
before the next shell sees to him.
Wounding, weeping from pain,

he will be able to see nothing.
And you will always mourn him.
You will write a poem.
You will count him into your dreams.

The other side of the sky's dark room

On the other side of the sky's dark room
a monstrous finger
of lightning plays war.

As clay quivers
beaded with moisture
where the spade slices it

the night quivers.
Late, towards midnight, a door slams
on the other side of the sky's dark room.

The spade stretchers
raw earth, helpless to ease
the dark, inward explosion.

Convolvulus

I love these flowers that lie in the dust.
We think the world is what we wish it is,
we think that where we say flowers, there will be flowers,
where we say bombs, there will be nothing
until we turn to reconstruction.
But here on the ground, in the dust
is the striped, lilac convolvulus.

Believe me, how fragrant it is,
the flower of coming up from the beach.
There in the dust the convolvulus squeezes itself shut.
You go by, you see nothing, you are tired
from that last swim too late in the evening.

Where we say bombs, there will be bombs.
The only decision is where to plant them –
these flowers that grow at the whim of our fingers –
but not the roving thread of the convolvulus,
spun from a source we cannot trace.

Below, at the foot of the cliff
the sea laps up the apron of sand
which was our day's home. Where we said land
water has come, where we said flower
and snapped our fingers, there came nothing.

I love these flowers that lie in the dust
barefaced at noon, candid convolvulus
lilac and striped and flattened underfoot.
Crushed, they breathe out their honey, and slowly
come back to themselves in the balm of the night.
But a lumber of engines grows in the seaward sky –
how huge the engines, huge the shadow of planes.

The grey lilo

The grey lilo with scarlet and violet
paintballed into its hollows, on which
my daughter floats, from which her delicate wrist
angles, while her hand sculls the water,

the grey lilo where my daughter floats,
her wet hair smooth to her skull,
her eyes closed, their dark lashes
protecting her from the sky's envy
of their sudden, staggering blue,

the grey lilo, misted with condensation,
idly shadows the floor of the pool
as if it had a journey to go on –
but no, it is only catching the echo
of scarlet and violet geraniums,

and my daughter is only singing
under her breath, and the time that settles
like yellow butterflies, is only
just about to move on –

Yellow butterflies

They are the sun's fingerprints on grey pebbles
two yards from the water,
dabbed on the eucalyptus, the olive,
the cracked pot of marigolds,
and now they pulse again, sucking
dry the wild thyme,

or on a sightless bird, not yet buried
they feast a while.

If they have a name, these yellow butterflies,
they do not want it; they know what they are,
quivering, sated, and now once more
printing sun, sun, and again sun
in the olive hollows.

Plume

If you were to reach up your hand,
if you were to push apart the leaves
turning aside your face like one who looks
not at the sun but where the sun hides –
there, where the spider scuttles
and the lizard whips out of sight –

if you were to search
with your small, brown, inexperienced hands
among the leaves that shield the fire of the fruit
in a vault of shadow, if you were to do it
you'd be allowed, for this is your planet
and you are new on it,

if you were to reach inside the leaves
and cup your hands as the fruit descends
like a balloon on the fields of evening
huffing its orange plume
one last time, as the flight ends
and the fruit stops growing –

Odysseus

For those who do not write poems
but have the cause of poems in them:
this thief, sly as Odysseus
who puts out from Albanian waters
into the grape-dark Ionian dawn,
his dirty engine coughing out puffs of black,
to maraud, as his ancestors taught him,
the soft villas of the south –

The blue garden

'Doesn't it look peaceful?' someone said
as our train halted on the embankment
and there was nothing to do but stare
at the blue garden.

Blue roses slowly opened,
blue apples glistened
beneath the spreading peacock of leaves.

The fountain spat jets of pure Prussian
the decking was made with fingers of midnight
the grass was as blue as Kentucky.

Even the children playing
in their ultramarine paddling-pool
were touched by a cobalt Midas

who had changed their skin
from the warm colours of earth
to the azure of heaven.

'Don't they look happy?' someone said,
as the train manager apologised
for the inconvenience caused to our journey,

and yes, they looked happy.
Didn't we wish we were in the blue garden
soaked in the spray of the hose-snake,

didn't we wish we could dig in the indigo earth
for sky-coloured potatoes,
didn't we wish our journey was over

and we were free to race down the embankment
and be caught up in the blue, like those children
who shrank to dots of cerulean
as our train got going.

Violets

Sometimes, but rarely, the ancestors
who set my bones, and that kink
where my parting won't stay straight – strangers
whose blood beats like mine –
call out for flowers
after the work of a lifetime.

Many lifetimes, and I don't know them –
the pubs they kept, the market stalls they abandoned,
the cattle driven and service taken,
the mines and rumours and disappearances
of men gone looking for work.

If they left papers, these have dissolved.
Maybe on census nights they were walking
from town to town, on their way elsewhere.
Where they left their bones, who knows.

I can call them up, but they won't answer.
They want the touch of other hands, that rubbed
their quick harsh lives to brightness.
They have no interest in being ancestors.
They have given enough.

But this I know about: a bunch of violets
laid on a grave, and a woman walking,
and black rain falling on the headstone
of 'the handsomest man I've ever seen'.

The rowan

(in memory of Michael Donaghy)

The rowan, weary of blossoming
is thick with berries now, in bronze September
where the sky has been left to harden,
hammered, ground down
to fine metal, blue-tanned.

In the nakedness beneath the rowan
grow pale cyclamen
and autumn crocus, bare-stemmed.
Beaten, fragile, the flowers still come
eager for blossoming.

Weary of blossoming, the rowan
holds its blood-red tattoo of berries.
No evil can cross this threshold.
The rowan, the lovely rowan
will bring protection.

Barnoon

We are the grown-ups, they the children
sent to bed while the sun is shining,
with a quilt to keep them warm.

We are the clothed, and they the naked.
Their dress of flesh has slipped off.
If they had a shroud, it has rotted.

We are old beside the purity of their hope,
those drowned mariners
anchored in salvation,

we bring nothing but a stare
of fickle, transient wonder,
but they make their own flowers –

a flush of primroses,
dog violets, foxgloves
taller than children, rusty montbretia –

and at Christmas they give birth
to the first daffodils
startled from the earth.

Getting into the car

No, they won't gather their white skirts
before stooping to enter
the deep-buttoned wedding car,

having placed their flowers
in the bridesmaid's fingers,
hand-tied, unravelling.

They won't wipe the delicate sweat
of condensation, and wave
one last time,

no, not for them the fat-tyred Mercedes
or mothers swooping to bless
with tweaks and kisses.

How the wedding car smells of skin
and heat, and dry-cleaning of suits –
but no, it will not happen.

Girls, it is your fortune
to be outside a club at 3 A.M.
to be spangled and beautiful

but to pick the wrong men,
to get into the car with them
and go where they are going

over the black river, under the black river
where your eyes will be wiped of sight
and your bodies of breathing.

Glad of these times

Driving along the motorway
swerving the packed lanes
I am glad of these times.

Because I did not die in childbirth
because my children will survive me
I am glad of these times.

I am not hungry, I do not curtsey,
I lock my door with my own key
and I am glad of these times,

glad of central heating and cable TV
glad of e-mail and keyhole surgery
glad of power showers and washing machines,

glad of polio inoculations
glad of three weeks' paid holiday
glad of smart cards and cashback,

glad of twenty types of yoghurt
glad of cheap flights to Prague
glad that I work.

I do not breathe pure air or walk green lanes,
see darkness, hear silence,
make music, tell stories,

tend the dead in their dying
tend the newborn in their birthing,
tend the fire in its breathing,

but I am glad of my times,
these times, the age
we feel in our bones, our rage

of tyre music, speed
annulling the peasant graves
of all my ancestors,

glad of my hands on the wheel
and the cloud of grit as it rises
where JCBs move motherly
widening the packed motorway.

Off-script

No, not a demonstration,
but each of us refusing

to learn our part.
The chorus dissolves
in ragged voices.

There is nothing for the director to work with.
We are quietly talking
off-script to one another –
'Yes, rhubarb with ginger – '

'Indeed we are all made from the dust of stars'

They are building houses
on rainwet fields
where the smoke of horses
has barely cleared –

indeed we are all made from the dust of stars,
even these houses are made from the dust of stars
whose light gallops towards us –

in the remotest corner
of the black-wet universe
there is a galaxy
of bright horses –

Tulip

How cool the lovely bulb of your roundness.
Bare-faced and sleek, you rise from your leaves.

You have the skin of a raindrop.
Blink, and your green flushes scarlet.

Poised on the catwalk of spring, you'll move
in your own time, smile when you want to.

Nothing comes up to you. Forget-me-nots
crowd at your roots, my fingers

hover, narcissi rustle
but you are still. Only the sun touches you.

Finger by finger it opens your petals
loosens the lovely bulb of your roundness,

makes you swagger in your exposure,
knows, as you don't, that it can't last long.

Beautiful today the

banana plants, camellia, echium, wild garlic flower's
rank tang of a more northern spring,
beautiful today the surf on Porthkidney Beach
and the standing out of the lighthouse, sheer
because of the rain past, the rain to come, the rain
that has brought this cliff-side to jungle thickness.

The hammock's green with a winter of rain, beautiful today
the bamboo, wrist-thick. Was it on this
foothold, this shelf, this terrace, it learned
to surf on a hiss of breeze, was it today
that taught this dry handshake of leaves
against the pull of tide on Porthkidney Beach?

A step, a seat, a stare to the east
where light springs from a wasteland
beyond where the wet sun dawns –
beautiful today, sun shakes from its shoulders
the night tides. In a wasteland of easterly light
sun makes play on the waves

but the hollow surf turns over and over
and nobody comes, only a track of footprints
runs to the sea, and the tall pines
make shapes of their limbs – beautiful today
the dazzle they capture as landscape,
the resin they ooze from their wounds.

White planks are full of washed-away footsteps, beautiful
today the graining of sweat and flesh. This shell
wears at its heart a coil
to last when the curves are gone – but today
the flush of light, the flowering of freckles
on tender skin are helplessly present

in the hour between pallor and sunburn,
while the banana plant wears its heart in a fist
of tiny fruit that will never ripen or open.
In the distance, the little town
waits for its saint to sail in on a leaf
for the second time, and bless its legion of roofs.

Dead gull on Porthmeor

You could use his wing as a fan
to rid yourself of dreams,

you could light a candle at midnight
in the flooded beach hut

and hear the wooden flute
waver its music

like a drop of rain
into a storm,

and the sea would prowl
along the black-wet horizon

and the sand would shine
as white as corn

ready for winnowing.
Yes, you could use his wing as a fan.

Narcissi

Everything changes to black and white –
the shaggy wreck of the Alba,
the shine of the neap tide

where the drowned funnels gulp for air
and the waves break like narcissi,

or the dog that skids to a stop, then quivers
all over, shaking a floss of water
to hide the Island.

The sea begins to smell of flowers
as the tide turns from its lair,

the narcissi flake off one by one
from that rust-bucket slumped in the sand –
the Alba's an old hand at drowning.

I was two when they first plumped me down
between Man's Head and the Island
where fox-trails of water ran out
over Porthmeor strand.

I smell something which reminds me
of not being born,
my mother walks on the shoreline

a figure or maybe a figurehead
with a smile of wood.

In the big glare of the white day
I clutch at the sand's
talkative hiss of grains,

lose my balance, and suddenly
scud on all fours
into the narcissi.

Dolphins whistling

Yes, we believed that the oceans were endless
surging with whales, serpents and mermaids,
demon-haunted and full of sweet voices
to lure us over the edge of the world,

we were conquerors, pirates, explorers, vagabonds
war-makers, sea-rovers, we ploughed
the wave's furrow, made maps
that led others to the sea's harvest

and sometimes we believed we heard dolphins whistling,
through the wine-dark waters we heard dolphins whistling.

We were restless and the oceans were endless,
rich in cod and silver-scaled herring
so thick with pilchard we dipped in our buckets
and threw the waste on the fields to rot,

we were mariners, fishers of Iceland, Newfoundlanders
fortune-makers, sea-rovers, we ploughed
the wave's furrow and earned our harvest
hungrily trawling the broad waters,

and sometimes we believed we heard dolphins whistling,
through blue-green depths we heard dolphins whistling.

The catch was good and the oceans were endless
so we fed them with run-off and chemical rivers
pair-fished them, scoured the sea-bed for pearls
and searched the deep where the sperm-whale plays,

we were ambergris merchants, fish farmers, cod-bank strippers
coral-crushers, reef-poisoners, we ploughed
the sea's furrow and seized our harvest
although we had to go far to find it

for the fish grew small and the whales were strangers,
coral was grey and cod-banks empty,
algae bloomed and the pilchards vanished
while the huer's lookout was sold for a chalet,

145

and the dolphins called their names to one another
through the dark spaces of the water
as mothers call their children at nightfall
and grow fearful for an answer.

We were conquerors, pirates, explorers, vagabonds
war-makers, sea-rovers, we ploughed
the wave's furrow, drew maps
to leads others to the sea's harvest,

and we believed that the oceans were endless
and we believed we could hear the dolphins whistling.

Borrowed light

Such a connoisseur of borrowed light!
Pale as a figurehead, undismayed
by the rough footpath
you climbed towards the view.

At the top, silent, you would breathe in
the spread of land you didn't care to own,
your face for a moment stern
and rapt, careless of children.

Such a connoisseur of borrowed light!
Even when your voice grew harsh
as those small stones rattling
down the adder path,

or when a January wind
harried cloud shadows
over the built-up valleys
you would climb as far as that boulder

where the view began,
and watch its unravelling.
You met equally
the landscape knitting itself

from russet, indigo
and crawling tractors,
or the blinding stare of the sea.

A winter imagination

Surely it's not too much to ask
from a winter imagination:

the clattering of chairs onto a pavement
the promptness of waiters before days waste them

and of course, the flickering of leaves,
the insouciant, constant

rapture of following the breeze.
Last night my daughter dreamed

that we would die, mother and father
gone while she stood watching.

I soothed her in my arms, promised her husband,
babies, troops of friends:

like the defences of a vulnerable kingdom
I named them, one by one. She slept rosily

but for me the bone-cold passages
still rang to her cry

You'll die and I'll be alone.

Surely it's not too much to ask
for a warm day to take away such dreams

for violet, midge-haunted shadows
under the sycamore that grows like a weed,

for this year's beautiful girls
to flaunt their bellies, while the boys

who won't stop talking, trot to keep up.
One of them is after my daughter

but her lovely eyes are blue with distance.
She is off at the gallop, dreamless.

Athletes

And what a load of leaf
there was on the trees by June.
From sticky fists
rammed in the eye of the bud
they'd opened wide,
and when the wind blew
the horse chestnuts were athletes
running with torches of green
in the half-marathon of summer.

Pneumonia

on our raft
after the long night of storm

the water bubbles
the sea is calm

the planks squeak lazily
where the ropes chafe them

the sea bulges
ready to open

why it should smell like jonquils
no one knows

the idling of the sun
changes everything

on our raft
after the long night of storm

the water bubbles
eye-level
why not watch it for ever

Wall is the book

(for Anne Stevenson)

Wall is the book of these old lands
each page scripted by stones,
each lichen frond, orange or golden,
wall's stubborn illumination.

Read wall slowly, for it takes time
to grasp the sentence of stone.
Wall breaks in a tumbled caesura
of boulders. Read on

where pucker of breeze on a tarn's shield
breaks the mirror of wall
and bog cotton trembles. It rains
on a draggle of sheep in the field

where wall breaks the force
and bite of steel from the north
whence weather and danger come.
Wall is the holy book of these old lands
each age scripted by stone.

Gorse

All through sour soil the gorse thrusts.
It is rough furze first, chopped to free the fields.
Burned off in sheets of carbon, it lives
down at the roots, grappling peat sponge,
black as an eclipse of the sun.

But when the gorse is out of blossom
kissing is then out of fashion.
Like ill-fitting shoes, gorse flowers
pinch and pinch until the sun touches them.

Now in the lanes a spice of coconut,
now the gorse thriving to wipe
the eye of winter with a cloth of gold,
now the bees in their bee kitchen

pilot themselves above the spines,
burrow past rapiers
bumbling, lunge into flowers
like drunks strangely kept safe
in a world full of harms,

and now it comes –
a prickle of intricate buds
a breath of perfume,
a flare along the roadways, a torch
barely mastered in the runner's arms
leaping the verges to set April alight.

Blackberries after Michaelmas

These blackberries belong to the devil.
Don't try to eat them now
or drop them in your pail.
Their flaccid sweetness

belongs to the one who ruined Adam,
set him to work in these hard fields
set him wallowing in green water
for pilchard and mackerel.

These blackberries are the devil's
and have his spit on them –
look where it settles.

To my nine-year-old self

You must forgive me. Don't look so surprised,
perplexed, and eager to be gone,
balancing on your hands or on the tightrope.
You would rather run than walk, rather climb than run
rather leap from a height than anything.

I have spoiled this body we once shared.
Look at the scars, and watch the way I move,
careful of a bad back or a bruised foot.
Do you remember how, three minutes after waking
we'd jump straight out of the ground floor window
into the summer morning?

That dream we had, no doubt it's as fresh in your mind
as the white paper to write it on.
We made a start, but something else came up –
a baby vole, or a bag of sherbet lemons –
and besides, that summer of ambition
created an ice-lolly factory, a wasp trap
and a den by the cesspit.

I'd like to say that we could be friends
but the truth is we have nothing in common
beyond a few shared years. I won't keep you then.
Time to pick rosehips for tuppence a pound,
time to hide down scared lanes
from men in cars after girl-children.

or to lunge out over the water
on a rope that swings from that tree
long buried in housing –
but no, I shan't cloud your morning. God knows
I have fears enough for us both –

I leave you in an ecstasy of concentration
slowly peeling a ripe scab from your knee
to taste it on your tongue.

Fallen angel

Waist-deep in snow and wading
through the world's cold,
this fallen angel with wings furled

on his way home from Bethlehem,
the story all told.
Centuries after the birth

through drab years with the promise fading
like gilt off the gold,
fallen angel still tramping the earth –

so long, the way back to Bethlehem
through the world's cold.

Bridal

Bride in the mud of the yard,
bare feet skilled to find
the nub of hard ground.

She stands as if she were transparent,
ears spiked, fingers encircled,
skirts stitched with metal.

Mud squelches through the keyhole
between first and second toe,
she slips, rescues herself.

Silence of banknotes
from sweaty hands, pinned to her dress
so the president's face shows.

She drives the cows in
through velvet of shit and slime,
their soiled tails switching

their dirty udders craving release
as women crave the gums of their babies
in the first shudder of feeding.

In the silence of the marriage night
with a befuddled bridegroom
too old for the task at hand
she will not cry out.

Bride in the mud of the yard,
thirteen and hopping
through velvet of cowshit
from stone to stone.

Still life with ironing

I love it when you look at me like this,
and the washed smell of your blue denim
We are washed out, the two of us,
shadows of what we have been.

A moth in the bowl of a paper lampshade,
a gust of night and a baby's cry,
a drop of milk on the wrist, inside
where the blood beats time.

Sometimes a heatwave is too much to take.
We are not up to it, up for it,
bare enough, blank enough. We fake
pleasure but turn towards evening,

to the clink of a glass, the settling of blackbirds
the talkative hose in the next garden,
a shirt with the buttons undone
and shadows put in by the iron.

Spanish Irish

It is your impulse I remember,
the movement that made you your own,
the way you laughed when you were told
some daily but delightful thing,
and the way you could not be fooled.

When I saw that man who recalled you
I put out my hand to keep him
as if his Spanish Irish face
must lighten in recognition,
and I was on the point of speaking
the pleasure of your name.

Cowboys

They rode the ridge those five minutes
I was caught in traffic
watching nothing but rain
falling on slate,

they rode the beauty of angles,
they laddered oblivion
and saved their own lives eight times
as their boots spun,

they rode without harness
astride the ridge of the roof,
they chucked a rope around the chimney
before it galloped off,

they rode in a rain-sweat,
they might have fallen like snow,
they hollered across the prairie
until the roofs echoed.

Below Hungerford Bridge

Below Hungerford Bridge the river
oils its own surface like a seabird.
Tide fights with current, crowds
surge to a concert, the light thickens.

How unaccountable the dead are:
I think you rear from your photograph
with an expression of terror: *I can't move.*
Will you let me out of here?

I think I see T.S. Eliot
wan in his green make-up
but slyly playful, a big cat
gone shabby with keeping.

The traffic halts. There's nothing
but a few pile-driven wharves
and the river remembering
its old courses.

Ophelia

I dreamed my love became a boat
on the saltings in winter
after long treading the green water,

I dreamed my love flew to the bar
where the tide teemed with the river,
and bucked and fought there,

I dreamed that my love's timber
was a bed for eelgrass
and marsh samphire,

I dreamed my love became a boat
on the saltings in winter
after long treading the green water,

and beneath his shroud of skin
was a rib chamber
for winds to whistle in.

Winter bonfire

My mind aches where I cannot touch it.
It has put a net over some words,
it is hiding a poem.

Who is that man tending flames in his garden,
and why does he heap armfuls of paper
on his winter bonfire?

If I write down anything
no matter how stealthily
the poem will know it.

One A.M.

Melancholy at one A.M. –
the poem ended
or else just quietly
lying under the table
gnawing the bone of its being –

the lighthouse in its bowl of sea
the town by its holy well
and the owls hunting.

Surf hollows the base of the cliffs,
owls hollow the safety of night
and the poem makes its rest
by turning and turning
like a hare in its form.

Lemon and stars

The stars come so close
they seem not to be shining
but to be remaking the world
in their own pattern

and we seem to be caught in their dust
like the fingerprints of creatures
not yet imagined.
Besides, there is the starlight

not enough to make star-shadow
but enough, in the absence of moon
to heap up darkness
just here, under the lemon tree.

Cutting open the lemons

After all they didn't taste of salt
or the winter storms.

I had not expected the insides to be so
offhandedly daffodil –

lemons should be more malleable
to the imagination –

but like babies they are sure
that the planting and tending

gives no right over them.

Hearing owls

The dark fabric of night not torn
but seamed with the flight of owls
hunting the margin of the Downs.

The houses pull their roofs over them,
the sleepers plunge beneath their bedclothes
at the onrush of wings,

the mouse runs with its trail of urine.
The owl pulls off a miracle
as it homes in

like a jump-jet in mid-Atlantic
sighting its landing area
in a waste of sea slop.

The mouse is done. The owl swallows
while a car passes, knowing nothing
of the owl agape at its own fortune.

'Often they go just before dawn'

A wash of stars covers the sky
before the day comes,
before the slippery quickness of brush-strokes
dries to a surface,

a wash of stars covers the sky
announcing with pallor
that they are going out
or that something else –

call it a day, or dawn –
is about to come in.
Quick, quick, get up the ladder
and paint in more brightness

for the stars to be dark against.

May voyage

A May evening and a bright moon
riding easily in its mystery,
you come out onto the balcony
and gaze there, relaxed, intent
as the horizon softens towards France
and the moon voyages, voyages.

What storms have you seen!
Such a hurricane
when wind hurled around the building
like an express train,
but you fought it out of your home
and now you note the turning of the tide
as the moon voyages, voyages

from peace into deeper peace
from old age into youth,
behind you the French windows are open
ahead of you only the shining
sea and the lovely work of the moon
as it voyages, voyages
into the calm.

Out of the Blue

(2001)

Out of the Blue

Speak to me in the only language
I understand, help me to see
as you saw the enemy plane
pounce on you out of the sun:
one flash, cockling metal. Done.

Done for, they said, as he spun earthward
to the broad chalk bosom of England.
Done for and done.

You are the pilot of this poem,
you speaks its language, thumbs-up
to the tall dome of June.
Even when you long to bail out
you'll stay with the crate.

Done for, they said, as his leather jacket
whipped through the branches.
Done for and done.

Where are we going and why so happy?
We ride the sky and the blue,
we are thumbs up, both of us
even though you are the owner
of that long-gone morning,
and I only write the poem.

You own that long-gone morning.
Solo, the machine-gun stitched you.
One flash did for you.
Your boots hit the ground
ploughing a fresh white scar in the downland.

They knew before they got to him,
from the way he was lying
done for, undone.

But where are we going?
You come to me out of the blue
strolling the springy downland
done for, thumbs up, oil on your hands.

The man on the roof

When my grandmother died my father eulogised her.
There she was, coming home with the pram
and her crowd of children
when something strange in the light
or its impediment getting at her from heaven
made her look up to see one of her children –
her eldest child, her son, him –

up on the roof, riding the horse of the homestead
with wild heels, daring her to defy him
and get him down. She got him down
with a word, as he remembers it,
her lovely penny-pale face looking up at his
from the path where her children swarmed and shouted
and it was this

he remembered when her coffin lay under his hands:
the roof, and his coming down.

When our priest died I remembered him
up on the roof, mending a tile
– a little job on hand, and a hammer
and air of busyness to keep him busy
while he pretended not to be pretending
to ride the roof in its wild beauty
over the unfamilied air of Liscannor

and half-way to America. Maybe.
Or maybe merely tapping the tile in
like a good workman.
'How beautiful it was up on the roof,'
he said to the people at Mass.

My father touched his mother's coffin
and did not say how golden her hair was.
Even I remember how golden it was
when the grey knot was undone.

Now they are gone into the ground,
both of them. They are riding on the roof,
their wild heels daring us to defy them,
and we are here on the ground
penny-pale and gaping.
They will not tell
how beautiful it is. I will not ask them.

Giraffes in Hull

Walking at all angles
to where the sky ends,
wantons with crane-yellow necks
and scarlet legs
stepping eastward, big eyes
supping the horizon.

Watch them as they go, the giraffes
breast-high to heaven,
herding the clouds.
Only Hull has enough sky for them.

Jacob's drum

This is Jacob's drum
how he beats on it   how he fights on it
how he splits every crack of the house
how he booms
how he slams
hair wet-feathered   sweat gathering
red-face Jacob throwing his money down
all on the drum   his one number
beating   repeating

O Jacob
don't let go of it
don't let anyone take your drum
don't let anyone of all of them
who want you to be drumless
beating your song on nothing
Jacob   they'd do it
believe them

it's time   they say
to put your drum away

do you remember the glow-worm Jacob?
how we looked and nearly touched it
but you didn't want to hurt it?
I thought it was electric

some trash a child dropped
some flake of neon
stuck to a rock

don't put your finger on the light
you said   and I stood still then
glow-worm   Jacob   remember it
I had the word but it was you
who told me it was living

and now I say to anyone
don't touch Jacob's drum

That old cinema of memory

O that old cinema of memory
with the same films always showing.
The censor has been at work again.
Is he protecting me, or am I protecting him?
This trailer's a horror, I won't watch it,
this one makes my heart burn with longing,
this is a mist of interrupted shapes
urgently speaking, just out of earshot –
experimental, I call it.

The projectionist should be on double time.
He's got a kid in with him, they're so bored
they play Brag rather than watch the screen.
The ice-cream girl's tired of pacing the aisles.
She rests her thumbs in the tray-straps, and dreams.

It's a rainy afternoon in Goole
and this cinema's the last refuge
for men in macs and kids bunking off school.
They yawn, pick their nails and dream
by text-message. Look at the screen,
it says CU, CU, CU.

Depot

The panting of buses through caves of memory:
school bus with boys tossing off
in the back seat when I was eight,
knowing the words, not knowing
what it was those big boys were murkily doing,
and the conductor with fierce face
yelling down farm lanes at kids as they ran
Can you not get yourselves up in the morning?

The sway of buses into town
the way the unlopped branches of lime
knocked like sticks against railings,
the way women settled laps and bags,
shut their eyes, breathed out on a cigarette,
gave themselves to nothing for ten minutes
as someone else drove the cargo of life,
until the conductor broke their drowse
in a flurry of one-liners,
and they found coin in their fat purses.

A lorry-load of stuff

It was the green lorry with its greasy curtain
like a leather apron,
backing into the lane behind the terrace
for a lorry-load of stuff.

Cardboard boxes of books from the last move,
not opened since. That's thirteen years
where *A Beginner's Guide to Birdsong*
and *Marxism Matters* have not been wanted.

Two plastic caterpillars, clattering
like tongues. They were new once,
expensive enough to keep for no purpose.
The boxes exist, though they don't fit.

A turquoise baby-bath, impregnated
with the white-knuckle grip of one baby
and the fat relaxed fist of the other.
One afternoon it served as a sledge

before the proper sledge, this one
(which we also don't want). Remember those woods,
and our stopped breath that headlong
downhill with both boys crammed in front.

A proper lorry-load of stuff
needs bits of wood, likely shapes
that finally won't hold shelves up.
It needs a toddler's bike

hand-painted silver by a nine-year-old
then torn apart to make a go-kart.
If there is old food (lentils,
tins with rust-spots, onion sets

that never got planted, or could be gladioli)
so much the better. In a climate too cold
for cockroaches, you can afford to be careless
of larder shelves. And your lorry-load

is incomplete without the photographs
you kept taking, badly, from duty,
interrupting the happiest moments
as you saw them. The booty

of time, it was going to be. Lose them
to the panting of the lorry's engine
impatient now, throbbing, and to the man
parting the curtain, chucking stuff in.

Virgin with Two Cardigans

There's a stone set in the car-park wall
down at knee-level
which commends her.

There are these relics: a scrap of wool,
a lost button, an unfollowed pattern.

There is her stone, set in the car-park wall
its flinty lettering so bright cut
it would blind her.

Here, on this path, slowly, leaning
on two sticks, she still comes.
Trying to know all the new faces
she looks about her, tortoise-sweet.

How patiently she wants God to unbutton
her two cardigans,
but he is slow.

Here, buttoning her cardigans
with lumpy fingers she bungles
in the lee of a breeze-block wall.

Virgin with Pineapple
Virgin with the Globe as a Golden Ball

Virgin with Two Cardigans
pushing a pearl button
into the gnarl of its hole.

Ice coming

(after Doris Lessing)

First, the retreat of bees
lifting, heavy with the final
pollen of gorse and garden,
lugging the weight of it, like coal sacks
heaped on lorry-backs
in the ice-cream clamour of August.

The retreat of bees, lifting
all at once from city gardens –
suddenly the roses are scentless
as cold probes like a tongue,
crawling through the warm crevices
of Kew and Stepney. The ice comes
slowly, slowly, not to frighten anyone.

Not to frighten anyone. But the Snowdon
valleys are muffled with avalanche,
the Thames freezes, the Promenade des Anglais
clinks with a thousand icicles, where palms
died in a night, and the sea
of Greece stares back like stone
at the ice-Gorgon, white as a sheet.

Ice squeaks and whines. Snow slams
like a door miles off, exploding a forest
to shards and matchsticks. The glacier
is strangest, grey as an elephant,
too big to be heard. Big-foot, Gorgon –
a little mythology
rustles before it is stilled.

So it goes. Ivy, mahonia, viburnum
lift their fossilised flowers
under six feet of ice, for the bees
that are gone. As for being human
it worked once, but for now
and the foreseeable future
the conditions are wrong.

Cyclamen, blood-red

Cyclamen, blood-red, fly into winter
against the grey grain of concrete
eight floors up.
Winged, poised, intricate,

tough as old boots
flying the kite
of pure colour

season to season
under a laurel leaf
they make rebellion.

Piers Plowman

The Crucifixion & Harrowing of Hell

(from the C text)

'It is finished,' said Christ. Blood ebbed from his face.
He was wan and pitiful as a dying prisoner.
The lord of light closed his eyes to the light,
day shrank back, the sun darkened in terror;
The temple walls collapsed into rubble
solid rock split, and it seemed black night.
Earth shivered like living flesh,
the dead heard, and emerged
rising up from their deep-dug graves
to tell the world why this storm was wrenching it.
'For a bitter battle,' said one dead man walking,
'Life and Death are wrestling in the darkness
and no one knows who shall be the winner
until Sunday, when the sun rises,'
that said, he sank down
a dead man, into deep earth again.

Some said it was God's own son who died so well.
Truly this was the son of God,
Some said he was a sorcerer, and practised witchcraft,
'Let's try him, find out if he's really dead
or still alive, before they take down the body.'

There were two thieves that suffered death
on the cross beside Christ. An officer came
and broke their bones, the arms and legs on each man.
But all shrank from laying hands on Christ.
He was King and knight himself, his nature God-given,
and none had the boldness to touch him in his dying.
Only a blind knight stepped out, holding his spear
that was ground keen and sharp as a razor.
He was named Longinus, and had been blind for long years.

Despite his protests, they pushed him forward
to joust with Jesus, this blind Jew Longinus.
No one else dared, of all those standing there,

to touch Jesus or take him down for burial,
only the blind man, who struck his lance through Christ's heart.
Blood leaped down the shaft and melted the darkness
that sealed the knight's eyes. As the light shone
he knelt and cried to Christ to forgive him
'It was against my will that I wounded you,
I bleed to think of what I have done to you.
I yield to your mercy. Do what you like with me.
Take my land and my life, they belong to you.'

For a while in my dream I withdrew into the shadows
as if I would sink down into hell's darkness.
There my sight cleared, there this was revealed:
out of the west a young woman came hurrying
gentle, benign, sweet-spoken,
compassion itself shining. Mercy was her name
and as she came she stared into hell's mouth.
From the east, as it seemed in my vision,
her sister appeared, lightly stepping westward:
she was virgin, pristine, inviolable Truth,
wrapped in such virtue that she feared nothing.

When they met, Mercy and Truth together,
they asked each other about these signs and wonders
the din and darkness, and how the day dawned
and how a glow and glory lay at hell's mouth.

'I am dumbfounded, dazzled,' said Truth,
'I must go and make sense out of these mysteries.'
'No mystery,' said Mercy, 'but signs of bliss.
A virgin named Mary became a mother
though no man touched her. She conceived by the word
and touch of the holy spirit, grew great, gave birth.
Without labour or loss she brought her child into the world.
God is my witness that my tale is true
and thirty winters have passed since that child was born
who suffered and died today, about mid-day;
it is his death which has darkened the sun
and made the bright world lightless, but this eclipse has meaning:
like the sun, man shall be released from shadow
when the light of life blinds the eyes of Lucifer.

The prophets and patriarchs have preached to us
that what was lost by a tree should be won back through a tree,
and what death felled, shall be death's downfall.'

'What friend of a friend told you that?' asked Truth.
'Listen to me. This is Truth speaking.
Adam and Eve, Abraham,
all their companions, all that are human,
all those prophets and patriarchs that suffer hell's pains –
that light will never be allowed to lift them up
and have them out of hell – Mercy, stop mouthing
and hold your tongue, for I am Truth
and I tell this truth, that hell holds them.
Read Job, and let him put you right by his ruling
that hell *allows no redemption.*'

Mercy, unruffled, answered her sister.
'I have grounds for hope, hope for salvation.
Poison drives out poison, the cycle is broken
Adam and Even shall find their redemption.
Of all venoms the worst is the scorpion's.
No doctor's skill can heal the site of his sting,
until the scorpion dies, and, held to the wound
drives out its own poison, turns sting to balm.
I would lay a bet with my life as stake
that this death will undo the deathly devilment
done to Eve in the earliest days.
And as the serpent seduced and beguiled,
so grace, which made all things, will mend all things,
and trick the tricksters by holy sleight of hand.'

'Let's stop all this,' said Truth, 'I see, not far off,
Righteousness running out of the north
from the cut of the cold. Let's argue no more
for she's the eldest of us, and knows most.'
'True,' said Mercy, 'and look, from the south
Peace dressed in Patience, dancing towards us.
Love has longed for her so long, I think it must be that Love
himself has written to her. His love-letter
will enlighten us all. We'll soon know the meaning
of this light that hangs over hell.'

When Peace, clothed in Patience, came up to them,
Righteousness curtsied to Peace in her rich clothing
and begged her to say which way she was going,
and whose hearts she would lift by the loveliness of her dress.

'I am filled with longing to welcome them all,'
said Peace, 'all those who have been hidden from me
by the pollution of sin and hell's darkness,
Adam and Eve and a crowd of others,
Moses and more than I can name. Mercy shall sing
while I dance to her music: do so, dear sister!
For Jesus fought well for them, and this is joy's dawning.
Love, who is my lover, has sent me a warrant
which declares that Mercy and Peace bring freedom
to release the human race from its prison,
for Christ has changed the nature of justice
into peace and forgiveness, through his grace.
Here's the warrant,' said Peace, '*in peace I will both lay me down* –
and to prove it is binding – *and rest secure.*'

'Are you out of your mind,' asked Righteousness,
or have you been drinking?
Do you really think that light there
has power to unlock hell?
Do you really believe it can save human souls?
When the world began, God gave his judgement
that Adam and Eve and their descendants
should die, and go down to everlasting darkness
for touching the tree and its sweet fruit.
Adam broke the law of our lord and denied his love,
by eating the fruit he gave up both love and law,
followed evil and fought against reason.
– by the letter of the law it is all over,
they must suffer for ever, no prayer,
no intercession can come near them.
They chose the fruit, let them chew on it.
And as for us, sisters, let's not complain of it.
That apple bite was a landslip
which changed their landscape for ever.'

'But I shall pray for them,' Peace said, 'for the end of their pain.
Joy and suffering are twined together so tightly
that one cannot be known without the other.
Hunger means nothing to full stomachs.
If all the world were like a swan's breast,
who would know what white was?
If night never came, what would day mean,
and if God's own tongue had not tasted death
how would he tell if was sweet or sour?
A rich man, living in health and ease
would never suffer, but for the death
that comes to all, equally, inescapably.

So God, who struck the light that began life
chose to be born human, to save mankind,
and be sold into death to feel the pain of dying,
which unknits all cares and ends suffering.

*

God placed Adam in peace and plenty,
God gave him freedom to sin and to suffer
to learn through this what his happiness was.
and God challenged himself to take on Adam's nature
and know human fate in his own flesh.
He came from heaven, lived on earth, and now
will go down to hell, and discover
the depth of suffering. The dark world
opens to Christ, who lived in heaven's light.
Christ will take the human race with him
on the same journey. Their descent into evil
will lead them to know where love is.'

'Listen,' said Truth, 'I see and hear it happening.
A spirit speaks to hell and bids it unbar the gates.
'Lift up your heads, O ye gates…'

A voice blazed from the light at Lucifer,
'Prince of this place, tear these gates open
for the crowned King of Glory to enter them.'
Then Satan shuddered and said to hell

'A light like this took Lazarus from us.
This is the moment of our undoing.
If this king enters, he will take mankind from us
and lead it where Lazarus has gone, and seize me.
Patriarchs and prophets warned of this
that such a lord and such a light would lead them.
Get up, Ragamoffyn, reach me those bars
from your Grandad Belial's wife-battering
and I'll stop this lord and his light.
Before this brightness blinds us, let's bar the gates,
check his course, chain our doors, stop up the chinks
so no light leaps in at the loop holes or louvers.

Ashtaroth, get the lads moving, the whole gang of them,
to defend mankind. They're ours, we'll keep them.
Hurl down the brimstone, blazing and boiling
to flay the flesh of those who come near our kingdom.
Set the crossbows and the brass cannon
and blind his troops with our ammunition.'

'Listen,' said Lucifer, 'I know this lord,
this lord and this light. From long ago I knew him.
No death can snuff out this lord, hell cannot cheat him.
Where he wishes, there he goes. But let him look out.
If he tears them away from me, he does it by force, not right.
For by right and reason, they belong to me
body and soul, the good and the evil.
For the lord of heaven himself promised it:
Adam and Eve and all their descendants
should suffer death and come to me for ever
if they touched the tree or picked the apple.
It was this same lord of light who gave the judgement,
and since he is truth itself, he must keep to it,
not tear from us what is ours, damned by justice.
We have had them with us for seven thousand winters,
legally ours, with no one arguing it.
Will he be untrue, who is truth itself?'

'True,' said Satan, 'but all the same...
You trapped them and tricked them, trampled down his Eden.
Against his law and desire you slunk onto his land

and caught Eve alone.
Woe to those who are alone!
And when you had separated her, you seduced her,
then promised them both they should become
as Gods with God, judging and knowing.
With treason and treachery you deceived them both
and brought them to break obedience through false promises.
So you got them out of Eden, and brought them here at last.
It was deception, not fair getting.

God will not be mocked,' said the Evil One.
'Watch out if you try to make a fool of him.
Our title deeds to their souls are false.
My terror is that truth will come for them.
As you mocked God's image in becoming snake
so God has deceived us in becoming man.
For God has gone about for thirty winters
in human flesh, travelling, preaching.
I sent sin to court him, and I asked him
if he were God, or God's son. He gave me a short answer.
So he's been out and about these thirty-two years.
When I saw what was happening, I plotted and planned
to stop those who hated him from martyring him.
I would have lengthened his life, for I believed
if he died, if his soul penetrated Hell
it would make an end of us all.

While his bones lived, he never rested
from his love lessons. 'Love one another' –
but the end of that love, and the aim of that law
is the end of us devils, and our downfall.

And now I see his soul come sailing towards us
in light and glory – I know this is God.
We must retreat, throw down our arms.
It would be better for us never to have been,
better to vanish from existence
than to endure the sight of this Christ.
Through your lies, Lucifer, we first lost heaven
and plunged to hell. You dragged us down.
We swallowed your lies and lost all happiness,

and now, because you had to lie again
and betray Eve, we have lost hell and earth
where we were lords and ruled everything.
Now shall the prince of this world be cast out.'

Again, that light bid the gates open. Lucifer answered
'What Lord are you?' A voice said aloud
'The lord of power and might, that made all things.
Duke of this damned place, now undo these gates
that Christ may come in, heaven's son.'
As he breathed these words, hell broke, and all Belial's bars.
No guard could keep those gates. They opened wide.
Patriarchs and prophets, the people that dwelled in darkness
sung with Saint John, 'Behold the Lamb of God'.
Lucifer blazed into blindness, and saw nothing
while those that our Lord loved flowed forth with that light.
'Here I am,' said our Lord, 'body and soul,
to claim for all the rights of body and soul.
They were made by me, they were always mine.
My law and my justice promised them
that if they ate the apple they should die,
but I never condemned them to hell for ever.
Their deadly sin came by your deception,
you got them with trickery, trickery took them.
You crept into my Eden in the shape of an adder
to steal away what I loved and looked after,
you teased and tricked them and destroyed my Eden.
The Old Law teaches that tricks will catch tricksters,
and truss them up in a web of deception.

Those that take life must lose their own lives,
the Old Law teaches. A murderer's life is exacted.
One soul must pay for another, the sin of my Crucifixion
wipes out Original Sin. For I am human,
and capable of making amends for human sin.
Through my own death, I undo death,
and I ransom all those crushed through sin,
and I trick the tricksters of hell through my grace.
So do not fool yourself, Lucifer, that I come against the law
to fetch any sinful soul by force,
but by justice and truth I ransom what is mine.

What was got with guile, is regained by grace.
As the human race died through a tree
so by a tree they shall come to life,
And your deception begins to turn
inwards, and stab your own flesh,
while my grace flourishes.
You have brewed bitterness, now swallow it.
Doctor of death, drink your own medicine.

I that am lord of life, love is my drink,
and for that drink I died today, as it seemed.
I do not drink from gold cups, or refined teaching,
only the common cup of all Christian souls.
But your drink shall be death, and deep hell your bowl.

After the great fight thirst grips me still,
my thirst for every human soul.
My thirst is so great that nothing can touch it –
all your spirits and rare vintages
will never slake it, till the grapes are ripe
and the dead wake. Ripe, and purple, and heavy-hanging
in the valley of the resurrection,
and then I shall come into my kingdom
and bring out of hell all human souls.

By right I will lead them out of this place,
all those I loved, all who believed in my coming,
but because you lied to Eve, Lucifer, you shall pay for it.'
And the lord bound Lucifer in chains.
Ashtaroth and the others hid in hell's crannies:
They did not dare even look on the lord
but let him lead forth whomever he chose
and leave behind him in hell whomever he chose.

The angels sang and swept their harps,
hundreds of angels poured out their music:
The flesh sins, the flesh atones for sin,
the flesh of God reigns as God.

Then Peace played these verses on her pipes:
'Glittering sun after rain,' sang Peace

The warmth of sun after rain-loaded clouds,
no love is sweeter, no friends dearer
than when peace comes after war.
Peace, armed with patience, puts an end to danger,
stills violence, destroys terror.'
'Truly,' said Truth, 'Here is the heart of truth.
Let us offer one another the kiss of peace.'
'And let no one say that we argue among ourselves,
for nothing is impossible to God,' said Peace.
'You speak the truth,' said Righteousness,
and she took Peace in her arms tenderly.
Mercy and Truth have met together
Justice and Peace have kissed one another.

They sang together in my dream until the day dawned
when the church-bells rang for the Resurrection,
and with that sound I awoke
and called Kit my wife and Colette my daughter,
'Get up, and honour God's resurrection,
creep to the cross, venerate it, kiss it
like the most precious jewel there is,
most worthy relic, richest on earth.
It bore our Lord's body to do us good,
and in the shadow of the cross
no ghosts can gather, no evil can live.'

Smoke

Old warriors and women
cough their glots of winter-thick phlegm
while a dog hackles for the bone
that the boy on the floor has stolen.

Whining, mithering children
in swaddles of urine-damp wool, prickling
with lice, impetigo and scabies, again
the toothache, the earache, the scabies, the glands
battling. Hush by the fire again
sing him a song, rock him again,
again, till he sleeps, still whining and wizening.

On the earth floor rocks his squat cradle
on the squat earth he has come to,
while one of the obsolete warriors
wheezes away at an instrument
made of sheep's innards.

He is a man of skills
learned painfully, not much of a singer
wheezing for the second time that evening
of the boar he killed with a dagger
of the bear with razor claws
that scooped out the face of his brother
then fell to his spear.

In song he remakes his brother
and their small play on the earth floor.
The baby cries. Smoke fills the hall,
the eyes of warriors and old women,
and nobody listens.

There's the skin of the bear on the floor
and a hearth gaping with flame
red-mouthed, then smoke hides it again.
By thirty everyone's teeth are broken –
look at that kid worrying his bone.

Bristol Docks

Ships on brown water
wings unruffling
masts steep and clean,

There goes the dredger,
there the steam crane
downcast, never used.

Tide goes wherever
tide goes,
forty foot rise
forty foot fall,
ship waiting
to clear Hotwells.

Time rises
time falls.
Two hundred years
shrink to nothing,

huge tides
shrunk to a drop
caught in a cup
where the men sip

tea, coffee
laced with rum,
talk venturing
westward, moneyward.

This is the slaver
money funded,
good money
from tradesmen's pockets,
guinea by guinea
fed into it.
Double it, treble it,
build on it.

Don't stare –
you'll cross them:
William Miller,
Isaac Elton,
Merchant Trader,
Merchant Venturer,
powerful men.

Edward Colston's
almshouses
(slaver panelled)
still standing.
Sugar houses
(easy burning)
all gone,
brown water
brown rum.

Custom House
African House
bonded warehouse
almshouse
sugar house.
Mud slack
licking its chops,
bright water
fighting to rise.

Look in their eyes.
They'll stare you down
for it takes guts
to get returns.
Investor,
speculator,
accumulator,
benefactor.

See their white wings
fledge on the Avon.
They speak of cargo,
profit-margins,

schools they've founded,
almshouses.

If you stare
at the brown water
you will see nothing,
every reflection
sucked and gone.

Slaver's gone
on savage wings,
beak preying.
Tradesmen's guineas
got their return:

coffee, cotton,
cocoa, indigo,
sugar, rum,
church windows,
fine houses,
fine tombstone
for Edward Colston,

the cry of gulls
goes after them
always lamenting,
always fresh
beaks stabbing
at their soul-flesh

The spill

Those words like oil, loose in the world,
spilling from fingertip to fingertip
besmirching lip after lip,

the burn; the spillage of harm.
Those words like ash, mouth-warm.

Without remission

Because she told a lie, he says,
because she lied
about the hands not washed before shopping,
she had to learn,

because he wanted her to learn
the law that what he said, went,
and that was the end,
and because she was slow
she had to learn
over and over.

He was an old-fashioned teacher,
he taught her hair to lie straight,
he taught her back to bend,
he taught silence
but for the chink of coathangers
stirring in the wardrobe.

He kicked the voice out of her.
There were no words left to go
with the seven-year-old girl
soiled and bleeding,
marched along the corridor

by this man, rampant
with all he had learned.
Later, locked up once more
she called through the door to her mother
'It's all right, Mum, I'm fine.'
But she was lying.

The rain's coming in

Say we're in a compartment at night
with a yellow label on the window
and a wine bottle between your knees,

jolting as fast as the sparks
torn from night by the wheels.
Inside, the sleeping-berth is a hammock

and there I swing like a gymnast
in a cradle of jute diamonds.
Outside, the malicious hills,

where to stop is to be borne away
in the arms of a different destiny,
unprotesting. Too sleepy to do anything

but let it be. So, that oak, lightning-cracked,
shakes where the flame slashes
and kills its heart. Swooshing up air

in armfuls its branches unload
toppling beyond the rails'
hard-working parallels. Say you join me,

say your eyes are drowsy,
say you murmur, *The rain's coming in,*
pull up the strap on the window,
the rain's coming in.

As good as it gets

She comes close to perfection,
taking the man on her thigh,
sweeping him home
in a caress of glitter, that way and this,

that, this, each muscle stripped
to bulge and give. See how her hair
streams in the firmament,
see how the tent

jutting with spotlights
puts one over her, then another,
another, a spurt of white
that slicks to her thighs

while the crowd claps time,
faster and faster, wishing she'll fall
wishing she'll plunge for ever
licked all over with glitter

love-juices, spittle.
Back she comes on herself,
her bird costume flaring.
As she lets him down

you see the detail: the rosin,
the sweat that follows her spine,
the sly, deliberate spin
with which he steps onto land.

But the crowd won't stop clapping.
They want her again,
they've been translated, they're Greek,
shouting *Die now! This is as good as it gets!*

If only

If only I'd stayed up till four in the morning
and run through the dawn to watch the balloons
at the Festival ground,
and seen you as your balloon rose high
on a huff of flame, and you'd waved,
and a paper aeroplane had swooped to the ground
with your mobile number scrawled on the wings.

If only I'd known that you were crying
when you stood with your back to me
saying that it didn't matter
you'd be fine on your own.
If only I'd trusted your voice
instead of believing your words.

If only I hadn't been too late, too early,
too quick, too slow, too jealous and angry,
too eager to win
when it wasn't a game.
If only we could go back to then
and I could pick up your paper aeroplane
and call you for the very first time.

Mr Lear's Ring

Mr Lear has left a ring in his room.
Is it of value, is it an heirloom?
Should we pack it with brown paper and string
And post it after him?

He hasn't the air of a marrying man
He hasn't a husbandly air.
No, his gait is startled and sudden,
And is he quite all there?

Poor Mr Lear has left a ring in his room
And it's not of value, it's never an heirloom,
But we'll pack it with brown paper and string
And we'll send it wherever he's gone.

Fortune-teller on Church Road

Two of us on the tired pavement
with the present pushing past
into the pungent smoke of the coffee-shop,

carrier bags stuffed with cargo
from Wal-mart and Tesco.
A tree of heaven, bright yellow

spreads its leaves above the peardrop
solvent scent of ASNU VALETING SERVICES.
She looks where I'm looking

this woman who asks questions
and tells me everything I've ever done.
For twenty pounds she'll give me a golden future

for ten pounds she'll give me a silver future
for a fiver a slam of bronze.
I believe in the glow of the leaves

in the shine of car-wax, in Wal-mart
and in the whiteness of her false teeth.
She would like to lie, but whatever possesses her

won't let her. Here it comes again
clearing the coffee-smoke, thinning the cargo
of carrier bags pushing past us,

until the Saturday men and women
lose their foothold in time.
Now they are the dead walking
at the pace of long-ago film.

Sleeveless

There he stands, blind on slivovitz,
eyes closed, face beatific,
propped against the side of the coach
while two girls rub him with snow.

He goes sleeveless in the snow
as if he belongs elsewhere
in a land where blood alone
is enough to warm him.

But this isn't spring. A hyacinth's
white whip of root in a jar in November
won't stop winter. The sun will go down,
the wolves will sample the woods

and snuff his footprints. But the engine's running.
Its vibration scrubs him awake
and those girls are laughing.
In ten long easy minutes
he will have left the summit.

The point of not returning

is to go back, but never quite back.
Through all those trees I am unable
to glimpse the house. Where the new road swings,
the dark lane made for footsteps remains hidden.
Where lilac-striped convolvulus
wound its scent in the dust, new road signs
describe the route in numeral and symbol.

There is the hill, but not the right hill.
There is a blood-red rhododendron
by a breeze-block wall – but not the right wall,
and those children in a sunburned straggle
who face the oncoming traffic (thicker now),
have bought the wrong sweets at the wrong prices.
They have too much cash: they are not the right children.

The form

Clearing the mirror to see your face
I'm sure you are there.
You came into the room behind me
but when I looked you disappeared.

Look. I am breathing out mist
like a horse in winter.
The glass I almost kissed
has gone cold. Now, is it you here

sitting in your usual chair
under the light, with your Guinness poured
and the best bit of the newspaper?
Let's have a tenner on Papillon, I'm sure

he'll do it this time. You show me the form.
I put out my hand for the winnings
and take the notes which are warm
from your touch. But the mirror is cold, sparkling.

The sentence

How hushed the sentence is this morning
like snowfall: words change the landscape
by hiding what they touch.
'How is he –? Has he –?'

Bridget takes off her glasses
and rubs the red pulp of her eyelids.
The world is a treasure-house of frost
and sparkling roof-tops. A few doors down
the sentence works itself out.

A roller-blader slashes the street like an angel
with heaven-red cheeks. A fag-end smokes
in the gutter where a dog noses. Such elation!
The labour of goodbyes
goes on quietly behind windows.

With short, harsh breaths

With short, harsh breaths
and lips hitched to each syllable
you read, but not aloud.

You rise and go to the stairwell
as if to call someone. Look up
at the whitish skylight, the peace

of another rain-pocked eleven o'clock.
You are here and you want her
but she'll come no more.

You keep her letters in a box
and deal them out like patience
to lie on your breakfast table

stamps obsolete, envelope eagerly torn
by the man who once lived in your skin.
You read the postmark again.

It's September, four years after the war.
Listen. She's speaking.

The footfall

It was you I heard, your tiger pad on the stairs,
your animal eyes blazing. Now you have my face
between your paws, tiger. It's time
for the first breath. Your playful embrace.

Suddenly you take away my texture,
the sheen I've had since I was born.
My hair. You comb it out with your claws
until the gloss and colour are gone.

My skin puckers slowly. Your whiskers quiver
as I keep still between your fore-feet
while you drink my juices, and for the first time
rake the lightest glissade down my cheeks.

Time for you, tiger, to do as you want.
I heard your footfall and waited in the dark,
expecting you. When will you come?

The coffin-makers

I can't say why so many coffin-makers
have come together here. Company, maybe.
More likely jealousy bites their lips
when they see another's golden coffin
where the corpse will fit like a nut.

No doubt they swap the lids about
at dead of night, scratch the silken cheeks of the wood
so when the mourners come to watch the hammer
bounce off the nails, they'll say it's no good
and in their white clothes they'll swarm
all over the coffin-maker like angry ghosts.

There's no need for it to be like this.
They could lend their tools to one another.
They could watch each other's little shrines
in case the candle goes out. Instead they blow it out
and sourly scour the insides of another cheap
deal coffin for the common man.
How many golden coffins can anyone want?

Of those who appear at the alley-end,
they prefer the advance buyers. It takes know-how
to select a coffin for yourself.
'In our family it's cancer. Allow for shrinkage.'
'Dropsy does us. Add it on to the width.'
Can a man know the shape of the wood
that will encase him? Can a woman
close her eyes and breathe in the scent of cedar?

These are the ones the coffin-makers like
to sit with by the spirit-lamp. For these they bring out
tea-plums, infuse *Silver Needle*
and drink before they do the measuring.
Time to compare wood-shavings,
rubbing their curls between the fingers. Meanwhile
man and wife from the flat upstairs
take their blue bird for a walk
to the evening park, still in its cage.

Inside out

Snug as a devil's toenail embedded
in blue liass, plastic
in your movements as in dreams, you kick
for headiness at the rich
red walls that close on you like elastic.

But now they've shucked you out, bare-naked
in the devil's kitchen, toes curled
flinching from chip scraps, ash,
lino sticky with beer tack,
the nail-on-nylon scrape of the cold world.

You are born, wed, dead, buried.
The wooden walls of your coffin
grip like hands, reassuring. You bang them
for joy that they'll bang back, booming
that you're hidden, hidden, hidden within.

The blessing

The halls are thronged, the grand staircase murmurous.
There's a smell of close-packed bodies, lilac,
hair-gel and sweat. Handprints on the brass railings
fade like breath on a cold window.
Outside the city is stunned with snow.

There he is, just where he should be
by that leather-topped, deeply-scored table
where fortunes are lost and made. He explains,
and those at the back lean closer
to catch the ripple of laughter.

A joke, and the group dissolves
to stare, study, and point a finger.
He waits for them to catch up with him.
You need a guide, with so many rooms
and between them, so many turnings.

I am there too, but not speaking.
I wait while the paint peels,
alone with the pulse of a Matisse
and the sunlight beating full on us.
But perhaps I say this

as I see him hasten down another staircase:
'You always had a blessing with you,
and you still have a blessing with you.
Keep moving. Go as fast as you can
and whatever I say, don't listen.'

Bestiary

(1997)

For Stephen Mollett
and Stephanie Norgate

...I was at home
And should have been most happy, – but I saw
Too far into the sea, where every maw
The greater on the less feeds evermore. –
But I saw too distinct into the core
Of an eternal fierce destruction,
And so from happiness I far was gone.
Still am I sick of it, and tho', to-day,
I've gather'd young spring-leaves, and flowers gay
Of periwinkle and wild strawberry,
Still do I that most fierce destruction see, –
The Shark at savage prey, – the Hawk at pounce, –
The gentle Robin, like a Pard or Ounce,
Ravening a worm...

JOHN KEATS
Epistle to John Hamilton Reynolds

Candle poem

(after Sa'di Yusuf)

A candle for the ship's breakfast
eaten while moving southward
through mild grey water
with the work all done,
a candle for the house seen from outside,
the voices and shadows
of the moment before coming home,

a candle for the noise of aeroplanes
going elsewhere, passing over,
for delayed departures, embarrassed silences
between people who love one another,
a candle for sandwiches in service stations
at four A.M., and the taste of coffee
from plastic cups, thickened with sugar
to keep us going,

a candle for the crowd around a coffin
and the terrible depth it has to fall
into the grave dug for everyone,
the deaths for decades to come,
our deaths; a candle for going home
and feeling hungry after saying
we would never be able to eat the ham,
the fruit cake, those carefully-buttered buns.

At the Emporium

He is the one you can count on
for yesterday's bread, rolling tobacco
and the staccato
tick of the blinds
on leathery Wednesday afternoons.
He has hand-chalked boards with the prices
of Anchor butter and British wine.
He doesn't hold with half-day closing.

He's the king of long afternoons
lounging vested in his doorway.
He watches the children dwindle
and dawdle, licking icepops
that drip on the steps.
His would be the last face that saw them
before an abduction. Come in,
he is always open.

Next door

is the same as ours, but different.
Back to front stairs, and a bass that thuds
like the music of demolition
year after year, but the house
is still standing.

When we have parties they tense into silence,
though they are good at fighting.
After the last screech and slam, their children
play war on their scab of a lawn.

We are mirrors of one another,
never showing what's real.
If I turn like this, quickly,
and look over the fence, what will I see?

He lived next door all his life

One year he painted his front door yellow.
It was the splash of a carrier bag
in the dun terrace,
but for the rest he was inconspicuous.

He went out one way and came back the other,
often carrying laundry and once compost
for the tree he thought might do in the back yard.
Some time later there was its skeleton
taking up most of the bin.

He passed the remark 'It's a pity'
when it rained on a Saturday,
and of a neighbour's child he said 'terror'.
He picked his words like scones from a plate,

dropping no crumbs. When his front door shut
he was more gone than last Christmas.
But for the girls stored in his cellar
to learn what it meant
to have no pity, to be terror,
he was there.

Under the leaves

How rangy they are, and lean, these leaves
tasting and licking.
These leaves are leaping
the intersections of Crewe Junction
on the back of the September wind
shushing along the sidings.

This is a place of rust, where murder
spurts and dies down, where spikes
of stilettos lodge in the points.
Not pretty, not. What we saw
when we opened the binbag was not
a resurrection of leaves.

This is a country of policemen, slowly tramping
a line that doesn't waver but vanishes
in teatime mist. Here the search
is begun, called off, resumed.
The tack of rain falling on plastic
will lead them home.

The surgeon husband

Here at my worktop, foil-wrapping a silver salmon
– yes, a whole salmon – I'm thinking
of the many bodies of women
that my husband daily opens.

Here he lunges at me in wellingtons.
He is up to his armpits, a fisherman
tugging against the strength of the current.

I imagine the light for him, clean,
and a green robing of willow
and the fish hammering upstream.

I too tug at the flaps of the salmon
where its belly was, trying to straighten
the silver seams before they are sewn.
We are one in our dreams.

The epidural is patchy, his assistant's
handwriting is slipping. At eleven fifteen
they barb their patient to sleep, jot 'knife to skin',
and the nurse smiles over her mask at the surgeon.

But I am quietly dusting out the fish-kettle,
and I have the salmon clean as a baby
grinning at me from the table.

Fishing beyond sunset

The boy in the boat, the tip of the pole,
slow swing of the boat as the wash goes round
from other boats with lights on, heading home
to islands, from islands: anyway they come.

Thirty-four bass, small bass, not worth keeping.
See them in the water, the hang
of twice-caught fish playing dumb,
then the shake-off of air. The kickdown

always surprises you, makes your feet grip
on the planks of the boat. There is the line
disappearing into the sunset
or so it seems, but it is plumbed

by your finger, which sees nothing
but a breeze of line running through water.
Behind you a sheet of fire
does something to pole, to boat, to boy.

Hare in the snow

Hare in the snow cresting
the run of winter, stretching
in liquid leaps over the hill,

then the wind turns, and
hare stands so still

he is a freeze of himself, fooling
the shadows into believing
he is one of them.

Need

(a version from Piers Plowman: *'The Pardon sent from Truth')*

I know that no one dare judge another's need,
for need is our neighbour, blood to our bone:
the prisoner in Long Lartin, the poor of shantytown
bearing children, burdened by bad landlords,
struggling to scrape together what goes straight out
on rent, on never enough food for the children
who cry like crickets from hunger, night-long.

They slave while they're sick with hunger,
wake in the damp of winter, crouch between wall and cradle
to rock the crying baby, their raw fingers
chapped with outworking, seaming denim
for half nothing, pitiful labour paid by the hour
which takes them nowhere, only to one more
half-hour's heat on the meter, scraping and struggling,
working for nothing.

The misery of women in run-down hostels
the misery of the men crammed in with them
racked by the nothing that is all they have,
too proud to beg, to show they are slowly starving
withering away, their poverty hidden like AIDS,
a shame that must never be shown to their neighbours
a shame that has made strangers of neighbours
and hunger the only guest at all their meals.

The world has kicked into me the future
of children born into poverty's welcome
to parents who have nothing but surplus labour,
empty hands, thoughts nobody wants.
Chips are their Sunday roast, dog-ends rolled up in Rizlas
damp down the parents' hunger as they look on
while the kids eat baked beans and bacon.
By the State's cold calculation
they could get by on carrots and bakers' leavings.
Only love can help them.

These will not beg, but there are beggars
who shoot up everything they're given
who have nothing at all wrong with them
who could perfectly well do a day's work
who deserve no pity, no money, nothing.
Even if they collapse on the streets, coughing
from the come-back of ancient diseases
think nothing of it. Don't be ashamed to walk past
with your wallet stuffed with credit cards
as the Bible says.

But yet. Look again. What about these beggars
who look perfectly all right, able to do a day's work,
ought to be cleared off the streets – all that? And yet
some of them come from another world, or another time.
Care in the community is the cold calculation
that takes care of them. Stop. Look again.
They live by the phases of the moon
by an inner fire that will not leave them alone.
They are penniless as time and tide, wander with nothing
like the holy apostles, Peter and Paul.
They have no time for preaching or miracles
but they can speak in tongues if you listen,
and catch the wind of truth in the sails
of what seems like play.

God who can do anything
might have made them businessmen,
but instead he made them his own children
and sent them out with empty bank accounts
holey jeans and a blanket to wrap around them.
These secret disciples break all the rules but his,
the one rule that tells us to love, and give.

Think. You will even put up with poets
for the sake of their patrons, if these are rich men,
publishers who fancy culture, and keep a newspaper.
Think of the Lord of heaven who has sent his children
to be called madmen, and please him
if you can, by throwing some cash at them.

And think again. When you are begging
for God's pardon, when the daylight after death
shines on your sins, think of them,
God's secret children, born pardoned,
and what you did for them.

Sometimes in the rough garden of city spaces

Sometimes in the rough garden of city spaces
where I believe a mugger will not approach me
because so far no mugger has approached me
I stop to take breath.
The city exists by acts of faith
that we and our children are safe,

that the pounding wheels of cars will miss them,
that the traffic will stop when the lights turn,
that parks will stay green, that money is not everything,
that the lime trees that line our streets are lopped and cropped
with the best of intentions,
that the orange glow of the streetlamps is moonlight
to that couple there, locked in each other, lost
in the city's night-time suspension.

I should like to be buried in a summer forest

I should like to be buried in a summer forest
where people go in July,
only a bus ride from the city,

I should like them to walk over me
not noticing anything but sunlight
and patches of wild strawberries –

Here! Look under the leaves!
I should like the child who is slowest
to end up picking the most,

and the big kids will show the little
the only way to grasp a nettle
and pick it so it doesn't sting.

I should like home-time to come
so late the bus has its lights on
and a cloud of moths hangs in their beam,

and when they are all gone
I should like to be buried in a summer forest
where the dark steps
blindfold, on cat foot-pads,
with the dawn almost touching it.

The scattering

First, the echo
at night, when I said
'I'll hold you'

and your voice like a bird's in the grey morning
came back 'Hold you',
and your feet in my palm
were barely hardened by walking,

and then the scattering,
the start of grammar
and distance.
You say, 'Hold me.'
You'll say, 'Don't hold me.'

All the things you are not yet

(for Tess)

Tonight there's a crowd in my head:
all the things you are not yet.
You are words without paper, pages
sighing in summer forests, gardens
where builders stub out their rubble
and plastic oozes its sweat.
All the things you are, you are not yet.

Not yet the lonely window in midwinter
with the whine of tea on an empty stomach,
not yet the heating you can't afford and must wait for,
tamping a coin in on each hour.
Not the gorgeous shush of restaurant doors
and their interiors, always so much smaller.
Not the smell of the newsprint, the blur
on your fingertips – your fame. Not yet

the love you will have for Winter Pearmains
and Chanel No.5 – and then your being unable
to buy both washing-machine and computer
when your baby's due to be born,
and my voice saying, 'I'll get you one'
and you frowning, frowning
at walls and surfaces which are not mine –
all this, not yet. Give me your hand,

that small one without a mark of work on it,
the one that's strange to the washing-up bowl
and doesn't know Fairy Liquid from whiskey.
Not yet the moment of your arrival in taxis
at daring destinations, or your being alone at stations
with the skirts of your fashionable clothes flapping
and no money for the telephone.

Not yet the moment when I can give you nothing
so well-folded it fits in an envelope –
a dull letter you won't reread.

Not yet the moment of your assimilation
in that river flowing westward: river of clothes,
of dreams, an accent unlike my own
saying to someone I don't know: *darling...*

Ferns on a hospital window

From behind the curtain an open window
fans the room with ferns of ice.
In this institution
health takes us by surprise.
We are tuned to a different station.

All night threads of cold make stars
like cells dividing on glass.
Behind me, monotonously,
Charlotte roars. In tinfoil, shaking,
they bring in another baby.

Long ago the ferns died into coal.
They give out their breath in sighs
fanned into flame, in pandemonium
hissing through pipes to this room
where a baby burns in my arms.

Diving girl

She's next to nowhere, feeling no cold
in her white sluther of bubbles.
She comes to a point like a seal
in his deep dive, she is sleek.
As her nostrils close
she's at home. See how salt water slides
as she opens her eyes.

There is the word *naked*
but she's not spelled by it.
Look at her skin's steel glint
and the knife of her fins.
With the basking shark
with the minke whale
and the grey seal
she comes up to breathe
ten miles offshore.

A pretty shape

I never stop listening to you sing
long enough to know what I think.
All I do is let it go on.

The bubble of song bounces towards me
over the wet surfaces of the kitchen
and you with your arms folded
in that tiny immemorial way you've observed,
your soft, small arms folded
over your chest where your breath
flows and unflows easily,
don't need to look at me.
The bubble of your song bounces towards me
its surface tension strong
as it shudders, recovers.
You let the song go where it wants.

When you've fallen asleep, or I think you've fallen
I withdraw, still singing
or perhaps still listening to you sing,
but you feel me going. Why am I going
always going, instead of listening to you sing?
Your hand knows better than mine
and with authority
of touch I cannot match
wraps me round you again.

Viking cat in the dark

Viking cat in the dark
is paw-licked velvet, sinew of shadow,
a thread of smoke bitterly burning,
a quiver of black like a riddle.

The huts lie low
a hoard half-hidden
a clutch of eggs
in the dune's hollow

and horned helmets
are nightmares to wake from
shapes cut from dreams
– but the cat leaps.

Like rain falling faster
the shadows whisper
and rain spatters
like death's downpour:

'Fight for me, dawn-slayer,
wake with me, sleep-sower,
keeper of dreams,
the dream we came for.'

There is no noise.
Only the quick
paws of the cat in the dark
like feet on the stairs,

but the cold grey hands of the sea clap
on the beached long-ships,
and a shape pours itself flat
to the chink of sword music.

Viking cat in the dark
is paw-licked velvet, sinew of shadow.
A thread of smoke, bitterly burning
quivers her body like a riddle.

Baby sleep

's
not like any other
day sleep   night sleep
long drive sleep
too cold   too hot sleep
What's that window doing shut?   sleep
get a bit of peace sleep
hungry   thirsty
need to pee
sleep,

baby sleep's
all over the shop sleep
new nappy and babygro poppers
done up to the neck sleep
fat fingers
starfishing
damp feathers
on neck curling
baby lotion and talc sleep
sleep in Mum and Dad's bed sleep
cry in sleep and then sleep sleep
sleep while the big peop
le wash and dress sleep
baby sleep

Frostbite

When you grow tired of the flame
wumping to life in the central heating boiler,
and the duvet sweats like obstinate flesh
in the middle of winter,

don't finger the lightswitch. Leave the coil
of electricity sleeping. Go down
tread after tread by the draught
of heat coming upward. The voice

of the house is warning. *Get out*
it breathes, *Leave us alone*
to our shuffling of dust-mites, our sorting
of smell and shadow into home.

First the bolt, then the chain, then the Chubb.
You're outside, but even in a nightdress
that comes to the thighs, you can't rub the warmth off.

Basketball player on Pentecost Monday

With his hands he teaches wind to move –
not this shuffle of leaves
from rows of pollarded trees
but the salt-laden, incoming
breath of the Indies.

He's six foot seven,
liquid in dull grey track suit,
his trainers undone.
There's a small keen boy
at his heels, yapping
for ball-time, air-time.
It's playtime in the gardens
with children sagely going round
on patient horses they strike with small
privileged hands.

Behind him, gravelly sand,
a guitarist picking
the bones of a tune
mournful as Sunday,
the empty horses
of carousels turning.

Tell the basketball player how tight
time is, how he's reached perfection
at the same time as the man with his rake
puts the gravel straight on something.
Tell him this is the moment
the arrow of his life flew out of
to return into his breastbone.
Or say nothing.

Tiger lookout

Refrigerator days.
Ours is the size of a walk-in larder,
casing everything.

One word
which has gone out of fashion
is *putrefaction.*

When Simmonds fell from his tiger lookout
it was not the growl
nor the stripes
that said *tiger.*

It was the tiger's breath.
All that old, bad meat
furring its teeth.

For a moment Simmonds was critical,
sniffing the exhalation of corpses,
the walk-in larder where he was going.

Tiger Moth caterpillar

Two spines curve in
as the sisters face on a gate
in their matching cardigans.

They are looking into something –
a stolen Swan Vesta box
plump with green privet,

and there's one match left
with which to poke it –
their marvellous possession.

Inner thighs chafe on a crust of lichen.
Riding the gate is the best game
these two have ever come on.

The more bloody a ballad
they more they love it. Cigars,
betrayal, the flames of hell

and the slaughter of innocence
are what speaks, makes the gate creak.
Girls, give us a song

in your tidy cardigans. Your hair's
deceptively sleek, you are
tangled, complicit, in on it.

Hungry Thames

Hungry Thames, I walk over the bridge
half-scared you'll whittle me down

where the brown water is eager
and tipped with foam.

You sigh and suck. You lick at the steps
you would like to come up.

Hungry Thames, we feed you on concrete,
orange-peel, polystyrene cups,

we hold our kids by a handful of clothing
to let them look at your dimples,

your smiling waters. We should hold them tighter,
these are whirlpools, this is hunger

lashing its tail in the mud, deep down
where the river gets what it wants.

The wasp

Now winter comes and I am half-asleep
crawling the hollow of an apple, my sound
a battery toy in a child's cupped hand,

or I climb to a ledge and lie, dulled
by its half-warmth. Half-wasp, I'm still
helpless not to sting your exploring finger

helpless in the pulse of my body.
The paddle of your hand churns
as you find something to kill me.

I keep on stinging. I cannot learn
through my crispness, the coat of warning
that says what I am.

On growing a black tulip

I was in the kingdom of pointed raspberries,
edible thistles, a green rose.
Everything was true yet false
like the yellow of whiteheart cherries.

As the tulips yawned it was simple.
The colour they call black is purple.
The veins in it are loaded, lifting
winter into a lamp of spring.

My dream was a hedge of tulips,
black tulips, glossy as swans
sailing the river of their leaves.
Next, golden delphiniums.

Little Ellie and the timeshare salesman

The man who gave little Ellie his forever
love was a timeshare salesman.
He let her look round the place
when the carpet was freshly steam-cleaned
and the teabag box was full to the brim,
but he left little Ellie for an instant
and she spied the used teabag jam-jar
sodden and rusty as iron.

Oh Ellie, whispered little Ellie,
there have been many here before you.
But she was smiling at the door
when he gave her his hand, wet from the ballcock
he'd quickly fixed in the cistern.
In a serenade of gurgles and yawns
the plumbing talked itself down
and perfect Ellie was his dream.

How could he replace or kill her
with her genius for noticing nothing
but the nice day, the short walk to the pool
the view of the beach from the bathroom window?
Sweet Ellie never crossed the time-share salesman,
but tended her one week like a garden.
She did not keep a diary where the others
might be noted or brooded over.

Kindly she watches him run on the wheel
of his weeks till he gets back to nineteen
where she is always happy to wait for him.
Dusty geraniums come back to life
in the days where Ellie waters them,
and the time-share salesman slackens his smiles
at the sight of Ellie's daring paëlla:
in week nineteen she is his forever.

Bouncing boy

(for Paul)

All the squares of trampoline are taken
by children leaping like chessmen
who won't play the game. Up, flying.
from tiny freeholds, hitting the sky's
elastic surprise, then down.

There's a space for you always.
Two kids eating ice-cream
with careful darts of the tongue
watch as you start to climb
the icy November sky, hand over hand.

You hear the clap of the sea
and your bright blue trampoline applauding
with the dull fervour of rubber
each time you go down,

and the kids eating ice-cream
with wind in their teeth say nothing
as the time mounts and your turn
grows impossibly long.

Ghost at noon

On the white path at noon when the sun
burns through olive and eucalyptus
and the pale stones rattle
as if someone's walking,

when the goat jumps and the sea shivers
like a dog turning its belly upward
to a hand that teases it,

and the sky is cloudless but suddenly
dark drops spatter the dust
and there, where no one is walking,
a line of wet footprints.

Crickets crackle in the dry maquis,
their sound unbroken.
No one is walking.
If you touch your finger to the dust, quickly,
you'll catch the pressure just gone.

Greek beads

Small, silvery, slipping
from finger to finger,
beads for street corners,

beads for white noon
when shadows curl by the walls
and the dog in the square lolls
with his tongue unfurled,

beads for navy-blue evenings
when the smell of oranges
drifts to the fountain,

beads for waiting on the landing-stage,
for the heat that shimmers
from village to village,

for the boy guarding the goats
and the old woman hoeing in black,
beads for leaving to find work
and for the dream of coming back,

beads for remembering
and for forgetting,
wrapped round the wrists of babies
and the dying,

beads for the life we live in,
small, silvery, slipping
from finger to finger.

Tea at Brandt's

Music plays gently. Yesterday's morning paper
flutters at the end of its long emigration
from being news. This is the present,

but when? Coconut cake, a stained napkin,
a tea-glass bisected by long spoon.
Any minute now it's going to rain.

What kind of animal is the past?
A wooden screen makes two rooms of one.
On the other side, where I saw her last,

my baby girl. I'll wipe her nose with the napkin,
take her to the Ladies and change her,
blow the bubble of words towards her
that says, *This is the present, there is no other.*

We are men, not beasts

We are men, not beasts
though we fall in the dark
on the rattlesnake's path
and flinch with fire of fear
running over our flesh
and beat it to death,

we are men, not beasts
and we walk upright
with the moss-feathered dark
like a shawl on our shoulders
and we carry fire
steeply, inside a cage of fingers,

we are men, not beasts,
and what we cannot help wanting
we banish – the barn yawn, the cow breath,
the stickiness we come from.

Recovering a Body

(1994)

To Virgil

Lead me with your cold, sure hand,
make me press the correct buttons
on the automatic ticket machine,
make me not present my ticket upside down
to the slit mouth at the barriers,

then make the lift not jam
in the hot dark of the deepest lines.
May I hear the voice on the loudspeaker
and understand each syllable
of the doggerel of stations.

If it is rush-hour, let me be close to the doors,
I do not ask for space,
let no one crush me into a corner
or accidentally squeeze hard on my breasts
or hit me with bags or chew gum in my face.

If there are incidents, let them be over,
let there be no red-and-white tape
marking the place, make it not happen
when the tunnel has wrapped its arms around my train
and the lights have failed.

Float me up the narrow escalator
not looking backward, losing my balance
or letting go of your cold, sure hand.
Let there not be a fire
in the gaps, hold me secure.
Let me come home to the air.

Three Ways of Recovering a Body

By chance I was alone in my bed the morning
I woke to find my body had gone.
It had been coming. I'd cut off my hair in sections
so each of you would have something to remember,
then my nails worked loose from their beds
of oystery flesh. Who was it got them?
One night I slipped out of my skin. It lolloped
hooked to my heels, hurting. I had to spray on
more scent so you could find me in the dark,
I was going so fast. One of you begged for my ears
because you could hear the sea in them.

First I planned to steal myself back. I was a mist
on thighs, belly and hips. I'd slept with so many men.
I was with you in the ash-haunted stations of Poland,
I was with you on that grey plaza in Berlin
while you wolfed three doughnuts without stopping,
thinking yourself alone. Soon I recovered my lips
by waiting behind the mirror while you shaved.
You pouted. I peeled away kisses like wax
no longer warm to the touch. Then I flew off.

Next I decided to become a virgin. Without a body
it was easy to make up a new story. In seven years
every invisible cell would be renewed
and none of them would have touched any of you.
I went to a cold lake, to a grey-lichened island,
I was gold in the wallet of the water.
I was known to the inhabitants, who were in love
with the coveted whisper of my virginity:
all too soon they were bringing me coffee and perfume,
cash under stones. I could really do something for them.

Thirdly I tried marriage to a good husband
who knew my past but forgave it. I believed in the power
of his penis to smoke out all those men
so that bit by bit my body service would resume,

although for a while I'd be the one woman in the world
who was only present in the smile of her vagina.
He stroked the air where I might have been.
I turned to the mirror and saw mist gather
as if someone lived in the glass. Recovering
I breathed to myself, *'Hold on! I'm coming.'*

Holiday to Lonely

He's going on holiday to lonely
but no one knows. He has got the sunblock
the cash and the baseball cap
shorts that looked nice in the shop
then two days' indoor bicycling
to get his legs ready.

He plans to learn something in lonely.
Bits of the language, new dishes.
He would like to try out a sport –
jet-ski maybe, or fishing.
You are meant to be alone, fishing.
There are books about it at the airport.

In the departure lounge, he has three hours
to learn to harpoon a marlin
and to overhear the history
of that couple quarrelling
about Bourbon and Jamesons –
which is the best way to have fun.

He is starting to like the look of lonely
with its steady climate, its goals
anyone can touch. He settles
for drinking lots of Aqua Libra
and being glad about Airmiles
as the Australian across the aisle
plugs into *Who's That Girl?*

Poem in a Hotel

Waiting. I'm here waiting
like a cable-car caught in a thunderstorm.
At six someone will feed me, at seven
I'll stroll and sit by the band.

I have never seen so many trombones
taking the air, or so many mountains.
Under them there are tunnels
to a troll's salt-garden.

The lake is a dirty thumb-mark.
If nowhere has a middle
this lake is its navel,
pregnant with sickeningly large carp.

Bent as if travelling backwards, the birches
wipe the cheeks of 29 parasols.
A little girl scythes at her shuttlecock:
4, 6, 7 strokes –

there are 29 bright parasols
outfacing the sun
and the little girl wears a red cap
to blunt her vision.

I lie through half a morning
with my eyelids gummed down,
neither rising nor falling
until the next meal comes round.

I keep a straw in my mouth
so I can breathe,
I am drinking Sprite in a hotel,
I am a carp in the reeds.

The Bike Lane

Of course they're dead, or this is a film.
Along the promenade the sun
moves down council-painted white lanes –

these are for cycling. On the other hand
the sea is going quietly out to France,
taking its time. If the cliffs are white,

iron stanchions are planted in them
so a bleed of rust can be seen
by the army rafting its way in

on lilos and pedalos. Professional cyclists
walk with one hand on the saddle,
waiting to be told to put on

red vests which show up in the race.
The aisle of the falling tide
squints to infinity, the bike-lane

is much in need of repainting
like the smile of the sea-front towards France.
In the less-than-shelter of the beach huts

two people I love are waiting
with as much infinity in their laps
as you can catch with a red vest on.

The cyclists flash past them –
one turns his keyed-up white face
but they are dead and this is a film.

Drink and the Devil

On his skin the stink
of last night turned
to acetaldehyde.
What comes through the curtains must be light.
It combs the shadows of his brain
and frightens him.

Things not to think of crowd in.
The things she said
as if sick of saying them.
The jumpy blanks in what happened.
The way he skidded and there
was the kid looking,

staring through the bars of the landing
so I shouted *Monkey, Monkey*
and danced but he wouldn't laugh.
Or was that in the club?
I would never harm a hair
on the head of him.
If she doesn't know that she knows nothing.

Ahvenanmaa

Breast to breast against the azaleas
they pitch, father and daughter,

the sun throws itself down
golden, glittering,

pale orange petals clutter their hair
as he catches her shoulders,

braced, they grapple and bruise
among the perfumed azaleas.

The flowers loll out their tongues,
tigers on dark stems

while breast to breast against the azaleas
they pitch, father and daughter.

The ferry slides between islands.
Pale and immediate, the sun rises.

The hull noses white marker-posts
glittering in summer water –

here, now, the channel deepens,
the sky darkens. Too cold in her dress

the girl scutters. Engine vents veil
steam while rain hides Ahvenanmaa.

Rubbing Down the Horse

The thing about a saddle is that second
you see it so closely, sweat-grains
pointing the leather,
pulled stitching and all, and the pommel gone black
and reins wrapped over themselves.
You see it so closely
because you have one foot in the stirrup
and someone else has your heel in his hand.
Your heel in someone else's hand

that second before they lift you, your face
turned to the saddle, the sweat marks
and smell of the horse, those stitches pulling
the way they tug and tear in your flesh
when you lie there in pain,
the hooves of it cutting,
trying to pin down the place, the time.
The nurse has your heel in her hand
yellow and still, already tender
though on Friday you were walking.

She is taking a pinprick
or else slowly, bit by bit, washing
your wrapped body from the heels upward
and talking, always talking.
She might want to ask someone
what way you would move when sunlight
filled the cobbles like straw,
or how without looking at it
you'd kick in place a zinc bucket
then bend and rub down the horse.

You came back to life in its sweetness

You came back to life in its sweetness,
to keen articulations of the knee joint,
to slow replays of balls kicking home
and the gape of the goalkeeper.

You came back to life in its sweetness,
to the smell of sweat, the night-blue
unwrinkling of the iris,
and going from table to table at parties.

Perhaps you'll waltz
on some far-off anniversary
with an elderly woman
who doesn't exist yet,

and you, you'll forget,
for now we're counting in years,
where we were counting in hours.

Heimat

Deep in busy lizzies and black iron
he sleeps for the Heimat,
and his photograph slips in and out of sight
as if breathing.

There are petals against his cheeks
but he is not handsome.
His small eyes search the graveyard fretfully
and the flesh of his cheeks clouds
the bones of heroism.

No one can stop him being young
and he is so tired of being young.
He would like to feel pain in his joints
as he wanders down to Hübers,
but he's here as always,
always on his way back from the photographer's
in his army collar
with a welt on his neck rubbed raw.

The mountains are white and sly as they always were.
Old women feed the graveyard with flowers,
clear the glass on his photograph
with chamois leathers,
bend and whisper the inscription.
They are his terrible suitors.

In the Desert Knowing Nothing

Here I am in the desert knowing nothing,
here I am knowing nothing
in the desert of knowing nothing,
here I am in this wide
desert long after midnight

here I am knowing nothing
hearing the noise of the rain
and the melt of fat in the pan

here is our man on the phone knowing something
and here's our man fresh from the briefing
in combat jeans and a clip microphone
testing for sound,
catching the desert rain, knowing something,

here's the general who's good with his men
storming the camera, knowing something
in the pit of his Americanness
here's the general taut in his battledress
and knowing something

here's the boy washing his kit in a tarpaulin
on a front-line he knows from his GCSE
coursework on Wilfred Owen
and knowing something

here is the plane banking,
the *go go go* of adrenalin
the child melting
and here's the grass that grows overnight
from the desert rain, feeling for him
and knowing everything

and here I am knowing nothing
in the desert of knowing nothing
dry from not speaking.

Poem on the Obliteration of 100,000 Iraqi Soldiers

They are hiding away in the desert,
hiding in sand which is growing warm
with the hot season,

they are hiding from bone-wagons
and troops in protective clothing
who will not look at them,

the crowds were appalled on seeing him,
so disfigured did he look
that he seemed no longer human.

That killed head straining through the windscreen
with its frill of bubbles in the eye-sockets
is not trying to tell you something –

it is telling you something.
Do not look away,
permit them, permit them –

they are telling their names to the Marines
in one hundred thousand variations,
but no one is counting,

do not turn away,

for God is counting
all of us who are silent
holding our newspapers up, hiding.

The Yellow Sky

That morning when the potato tops rusted,
the mangle rested and the well ran dry
and the turf house leaned like a pumpkin
against the yellow sky

there was a fire lit in the turf house
and a thin noise of crying,
and under the skinny sheets a woman
wadded with cloth against bleeding.

That morning her man went to the fields
after a shy pause at the end of her bed,
trying not to pick out the smell of her blood,
but she turned and was quiet.

All day the yellow sky walked on the turves
and she thought of things heavy to handle,
her dreams sweated with burdens,
the bump and grind of her mangle.

All day the child creaked in her cradle
like a fire as it sinks
and the woman crooned when she was able
across the impossible inches.

At that moment at the horizon there came a horseman
pressed to the saddle, galloping, galloping
fast as the whoop of an ambulance siren –
and just as unlikely. What happened

was slower and all of a piece.
She died. He lived (the man in the fields),
the child got by on a crust
and lived to be thirty, with sons. In the end
we came to be born too. Just.

Getting the Strap

The Our Father, the moment of fear.
He dodged round us and ran,
but was fetched back again
to stand before us on the platform.

The Our Father, the moment of fear
as the fist gripped and he hung
from the headmaster's arm,
doubling on the spot like a rabbit
blind for home.

The Our Father, the moment of fear.
The watch he'd stolen was given
back to its owner, dumb
in the front row, watching the strapping.

The Our Father, the moment of fear.
The strap was old and black and it cracked
on belly buttock and once across his lip
because he writhed and twisted.
He would not stand and take it.

The Our Father, the moment of fear.
There was a lot of sun
leaking through churchy windows
onto a spurt of urine.
After an age of watching
we sang the last hymn.

Adders

This path is silky with dust
where a lizard balances across bracken fronds
and a brown butterfly opens wide
to the stroke of the sun,

where a trawler feels its way along the sandbanks
and two yachts, helplessly paired, tack far out
like the butterflies which have separated and gone quiet.

A wild damson tree bulges with wasps
among heaps that are not worth picking,
and there a branch splits white with the lightning
of too heavy a harvest.

The lizard is gone in a blink.
Its two-pronged tail – half withered, half growing –
flicks out of the sun.
For a moment the pulse in its throat
keeps the grass moving.

A grass-bound offering of yarrow,
rosebay willow herb and veined convolvulus
lies to one side of the path
as if someone's coming back.
Instead, the sift of the dust –
beneath the bracken these hills are full of adders.

The conception

In the white sheets I gave you
everything I am capable of –
at the wrong time
of the month we opened
to the conception,

you were dewed like a plum
when at two A.M.
you reached under the bed
for a drink of water adrift
in yesterday's clothes,

our sheets were a rope
caught between our thighs,
we might easily have died
but we kept on climbing.

Scan at 8 weeks

The white receiver
slides up my vagina,

I turn and you've come,
though I'm much too old for this
and you're much too young.

That's the baby
says the radiographer.
You are eight millimetres long
and pulsing,

bright in the centre of my much-used womb
which to my astonishment
still looks immaculate.

You are all heart,
I watch you tick and tick

and wonder
what you will come to,

will this be our only encounter
in the white gallery of ultrasound

or are you staying?
One day will we talk about this

moment when I first saw your spaceship
far off, heading for home?

Pedalo

She swam to me smiling, her teeth
pointed by salt water, her mouth

a rock-pool's spat-out wine gum,
and then the tide flung

over her threshold,
and her lips moved.

The valve of her mouth was plumed
with salt-sweet tendrils,

sea danced from her pelt
of oil and muscle,

she rested her elbows on my pedalo
and there she hung

browning the pads of her shoulders
like a snake in the sun.

On shore thunderhead pines
drifted and swelled
like August umbrellas
stunning the fronts of hotels.

The sharp tide rinsed
over her threshold
as she dived once
and an angler cast
with lightning-proof rod
from the crinkled rocks.

A slow Medusa tilted beneath her,
shadowing toes and ankles
then on with its belly to the south,
braille on its tentacles.
She could read it like a newspaper
as it hunted alongside her.

I shivered
at the roll of her syllables,
and her joined feet winnowing,

and so I trawled her with me
over a shallow forest of dog-jawed
fruit sucking the trees,

past angler-fish socketing sand
with stone-cold faces,
through shrimps which divided between them
her armpit crevices

then flicked that way and this
tasting the dew of her breasts.

I trawled her past innocent sand
and the spumy outstretched arms
of agar and tangle –
but no, I wouldn't look down

however she called to me
until my fingers were shrunk
like old laundry.

I did not dare look down
to be snagged by ruby and seal-black
trees relaxing their weave.

On shore nobody's waiting.
The children, firm and delicious
as morning goods, have sheathed up their spades.

The boy with burned legs
has stepped out of his pantaloons
and skips in his blue vest
on the verandah boards.

The big one lights a mosquito candle,
Dad fills his glass of wine
four times, while they count,

and crickets saw in the ditch, frantic
along with the old car number-plate
and the boys' jar of fishing maggots.

They are screeching, all of them:
night, night, night's come
and no one's ever had a pedalo out this long.

Night-wind sifts on the shore
where striped recliners and wind-breaks
squeak by the green pavilion
crying for more.

I've lost my wife to the sea
Dad thinks hazily,
and takes another bottle of Muscadet
out of the gas cooler,

he imagines her dreaming
and sleeping miles from him,

each breath takes her farther,
toes in the air,

sea claps under her pedalo
impudently happy –

Below me now a mirror of wave-ruts
in firm brown sand,
I'd pulled her with me for miles
and there was nowhere to hide.

Now let me see you swim back
I said. She was mouthing
like mackerel tossed in a bucket
when the man's too busy to kill it,

with her scale-lapped bathing-hat
fly-blown and crazing.
She had nothing on underneath.
She was bare and bald as an eel.

Now she was an old bathing-woman
a mackintoshed marine Venus,
now she was that girl with lipstick
a push-up bra and a beehive,

now she was a slippery customer at Cannes
bare-breasted and young,
now she was my old
familiar snake again.

I took her curls in my hands and I pulled
but they were limpetted, smiling,
and there were just the two of us rocking.

We were close as spies
and she stayed silent
till day dived after its horizon
and the sea rustled with moonlight.

Swell shuts and opens
like a throat,

she claps
under my pedalo
impudently happy.

Where are you now
my sister, my spouse?

Clap with one hand
or clap to nothing –
I know you can.

Kiss me with the kisses of your mouth
my sister, my spouse.

The pedalo rocks
and is still again.

Beetroot Soup

Its big red body ungulps
from the bowl in the fridge
with a fat shiver.

Glazed
with yellow beading of grease
the soup melts from the edge,

yesterday's beetroot
turns the texture of tongues
rolling their perfect ovals
out of the silt at the bottom.

Like duck breast-feathers, the dumplings
wisp to the surface, curl
as the soup brightens
just off the boil.

There'll be pearl onions
– two to a mouthful –
white butter,
then later

plums
piled in a bucket
under the table
thatched with dull leaves
and a black
webbing of twig
over their round
sleep.

When the soup's done
yellow
constellations
burst on its skin,

bread goes to work
wiping and sopping

the star-scum
set in a slick

on the base of the pot –
chicken fat.

The Diving Reflex

Where the great ship sank I am,
where cathedrals of ice breathe through me
down naves of cold
I tread and roll,

where the light goes
and the pressure weighs
in the rotten caves of an iceberg's side
I glide,

I am mute, not breathing,
my shoulders hunched to the stream
with the whales, drowsing.

Bells rang in my blood
as I went down
purling, heart over heel
through the nonchalant
fish-clad ocean –

her inquisitive kiss
slowed me to this
great cartwheel.

Down I go, tied to my rope.
I have my diving reflex to sister me,
and the blubbery sea cow
nods, knowing me.

There is blood in my veins
too thick for panic,
there is a down
so deep a whale
thins to a sheet of paper
and here I hang.
I will not drown.

The diving reflex can enable the human body to shut down and maintain
life for as long as forty minutes underwater at low temperatures.

Bathing at Balnacarry

Two miles or so beyond
the grey flank of the farm
and the wall of gravestones
the oncoming rain
put an edge on the mountains,

they were blue and sure
as the blade of a pocket knife
whizzed to a razor traverse
cutting the first
joint of my thumb –

It was stitched, not bleeding,
the dark threads in the sea were weeds
and my son was packing them
between the stones of his dam.

He was holding back the river
while the mountain punctured clouds
to hold back rain
no farther off than we'd cycled
bumping towards our swim.

In the grey purse of Balnacarry
there were red pebbles and smooth pebbles
and the close grain of the water,

the men were absent –
one walking in the woods
one fishing off the rocks –

the child behind me built up his dam
through which the downpour would blossom
in the sea at Balnacarry –
it was cold, but not lonely
as I stripped and swam.

Boys on the Top Board

Boys on the top board
too high to catch.
Noon is painting them out.

Where the willow swans
on the quarry edge
they tan and sweat

in the place of divers
with covered nipples –
Olympians,

that was the way of it.
Boys in the breeze
on the top board

where the willow burns
golden and green
on feet grappling –

boys fooling
shoulder to shoulder,
light shaking.

The lake's in shadow,
the day's cooling,
time to come down –

they stub their heels on the sun
then pike-dive
out of its palm.

Sylvette Scrubbing

Sylvette scrubbing,
arms of a woman
marbled with muscle
swabbing the sill,

tiny red grains
like suck kisses
on Sylvette's skin,
Sylvette's wrists
in and out of the water
as often as otters.

She grips that pig of a brush
squirts bristle
makes the soap crawl then
wipes it all up.

Babes in the Wood

Father,
I remember when you left us.
I knew all along
it was going to happen.
You gave me bread but wouldn't look at me
and Hansel couldn't believe it
because you were his hero,
but I loved you and knew
when you stroked my hair you were bound to leave us.

It was Hansel who crumbled the bread
while I skipped at your side and pretended
to prattle questions and guess nothing.

Father,
did you drive home quickly or slowly,
thinking of your second family
waiting to grab your legs with shrieks of *'Daddy!'*
and of your new wife's face, smoothing
now she sees you're alone?

Father,
we love it here in the forest.
Hansel's got over it. I've learned to fish
and shoot rabbits with home-made arrows.
We've even built ourselves a house
where the wolves can't get us.
But wolves don't frighten us much
even when they howl in the dark.
With wolves, you know where you are.

Cajun

This is what I want –

to be back again
with the night to come –

slipper-bags across our saddles
how fast we rode
and all for nothing.

Your lips on his lips
your hand in his hand
as you went from the dance.

We heard Mass at dawn,
When I knelt for communion

it was the hem of your white dress
I felt in my mouth,

it was your lips moving.

This is all I want

to be there again
with the night to come –

meet me where the fire
lights the bayou

watch my sweat shine
as I play for you.

It is for you I play
my voice leaping the flames,

if you don't come
I am nothing.

Then I think how the train

Then I think how the train
from being a far blue point
troubling the slick of track
like thought in the dead of night
with a rack of stations between
the pulse of it and me

suddenly breathes at my back.
The platform stammers
and I see my poems
and see my youth in my poems
look up and back – then I think how the train

argues with a cloud of flowers
and always wins
cutting away with its cargo
leaving me in the carpark.

I tack the tarmac with footmarks
but now the train
switches its tail
shaking the rails,

then I think how the train
was waiting for me, a mushroom
put there for my hand
in the cow-coloured dawn.

That far blue point
how fast it's grown
having visited each one of the rack of stations
and found no one home.

How quick you are, I think to the train,
how near you've come.

Skips

If I wanted totems, in place of the poles
slung up by barbers, in place of the clutter
of knife-eyed kids playing with tops and whips,
and boys in cut-down men's trousers
swaggering into camera,
I'd have skips.

First, red and white bollards
to mark the road-space they need.
A young couple in stained workwear
– both clearly solicitors –
act tough with the driver, who's late.
The yellow god with its clangorous emptiness
sways on the chains.
The young man keeps shouting *BACK A LITTLE!*
as the skip rides above his BMW.
The driver, vengeful, drops it askew.

Next, the night is alive with neighbours
bearing their gifts, propitiations
and household gods – a single-tub washing-machine,
a cat-pissed rug, two televisions.
Soundless as puppets, they lower them
baffled in newspaper, then score
a dumbshow goal-dance to the corner.

Time by Accurist

Washed silk jacket by Mesa
in cream or taupe, to order,
split skirt in lime
from a selection at Cardoon,
£84.99,

lycra and silk body, model's own,
calf-skin belt by Bondage, £73.99,
tights from a range at Pins,
deck-shoes, white, black or strawberry,
all from Yoo Hoo,
baby's cotton trousers and braces
both at Workaday
£96.00; see list for stockists.

Photographs by André McNair,
styled by Lee LeMoin,
make-up by Suze Fernando at Face the Future,
hair by Joaquim for Plumes.
Models: Max and Claudie.
Location: St James Street Washeteria
(courtesy of Route Real America
and the Cape Regis Hotel),

baby, model's own,
lighting by Sol,
time by Accurist.

The Silent Man in Waterstones

> I shall be the first to lead the Muses to my native land
>
> VIRGIL

The silent man in Waterstones
LOVE on one set of knuckles
HATE on the other
JESUS between his eyes
drives his bristling blue skull
into the shelves,
thuds on CRIME / FANTASY
shivers a stand of Virago Classics
head-butts Dante.

The silent man in Waterstones
looks for a bargain.
Tattered in flapping parka
white eyes wheeling
he catches
light on his bloody earlobes
and on the bull-ring
he wears through his nose.

The silent man in Waterstones
raps for attention.
He has got Virgil by the ears:
primus ego in patriam mecum...
He'll lead the Muse to a rat-pissed underpass
teach her to beg
on a carpet of cardboard
and carrier bags.

The Wardrobe Mistress

This is the wardrobe mistress, touching
her wooden wardrobe. Here is her smokey
cross of chrysanthemums
skewed by the font.

They have put you in this quietness
left you here for the night.
Your coffin is like a locker
of mended ballet shoes.

You always looked in the toes.
There was blood in them, rusty
as leaves, blood from ballerinas.
Tonight it is All Souls

but you'll stop here quietly,
only the living have gone to the cemetery
candles in their hands
to be blown about under the Leylandii.

In your wooden wardrobe, you're used to waiting.
You know these sounds to the bone:
they are showing people to their seats
tying costumes at the back.

Everything they say is muffled,
the way it is backstage.
A stagehand pushes your castors
so you glide forward.

You know Manon is leaning
on points against a flat,
nervously flexing
her strong, injured feet,

you're in position too, arms crossed,
touching your bud of wood.
You needn't dance, it's enough
to do what you always did.

That was the second bell. You feel it
tang through the crush. The wind
pours on like music
drying everyone's lips,

they're coming, your dancers.
You hate the moment of hush.
There. The quick luck-words
knocking on wood.

When You've Got

When you've got the plan of your life
matched to the time it will take
but you just want to press SHIFT / BREAK
and print over and over
this is not what I was after
this is not what I was after,

when you've finally stripped out the house
with its iron-cold fireplace,
its mouldings, its mortgage,
its single-skin walls
but you want to write in the plaster
'This is not what I was after,'

when you've got the rainbow-clad baby
in his state-of-the-art pushchair
but he arches his back at you
and pulps his Activity Centre
and you just want to whisper
'This is not what I was after,'

when the vacuum seethes and whines in the lounge
and the waste-disposal unit blows,
when tenners settle in your account
like snow hitting a stove,
when you get a chat from your spouse
about marriage and personal growth,

when a wino comes to sleep in your porch
on your Citizen's Charter
and you know a hostel's opening soon
but your headache's closer
and you really just want to torch
the bundle of rags and newspaper

and you'll say to the newspaper
'This is not what we were after,
this is not what we were after.'

Afterword

Forty is a good age for thinking about the body. These poems were written in three and a half years or so between thirty-seven and forty, and if there is an underpinning web to this collection, if there is a conversation going on between the poems which is more than the sum of what each poem is saying, then I think it is to do with the body.

Sexuality, ageing, death, reproduction – these are all so much more relative than we think when we confront them first as absolutes in childhood or adolescence. At forty I find myself living in a time of almost overwhelming physical change. The first swathe has been cut through contemporaries by sickness, accident and death. Now ours is the generation that organises funerals: funerals of parents, funerals of colleagues and mentors who were thirty or more years older and have suffered that strange thing called a natural death. We have to watch weakness in those who were strong, and strength developing in the dependent. People in the rich West stay late-middle-aged for so long now. The years tick on and then suddenly, astonishingly, the world narrows to a white bed and the wink of the electrocardiograph. Our children are growing fiercely, claiming their own sexuality, taking up more room in the house than we dare to do. Their skin and hair and smiles bloom breathtakingly.

And those familiar bones in the mirror are covered by flesh which is beginning to change in ways I scarcely understand. No longer the youngest person on the bus, no longer automatically raked by male eyes in public places, no longer constantly made conscious of who I am and where I am by whistles and comments. *Go on darling, give us a smile.* Now I can forget how to smooth my face to unresponsive blankness in public or how to walk past building-sites with apparent unconcern. There's great freedom in this, and a powerful sense of recovering a body which for years seemed to belong as much to other people as to me.

The instability of the body is a source of comedy too. It swells and shrinks, presents itself one day as beautiful, the next as awkward and unsure. It sweats for fitness to stave off an autumn which is already wrinkling the edges of the leaves. It relishes an intimate, unshared life of snores, farts, bum-reducing exercises, masturbation and nose-picking, then walks out into public immaculately sheathed in whatever appearance suits it that day. The flesh-pinching reality of our bodies is constantly undermined by their surreality.

A late pregnancy has concentrated these thoughts in me. A woman of forty begins to look back on nearly thirty years of menstrual cycles, of the fear of pregnancy or the hope of pregnancy, of being always somewhere in a hormonal pattern which is both private and socially significant. Ahead of her is the menopause with its promise of a stability not experienced since childhood. And yet suddenly the body proves itself fertile again, capable of re-engaging in that flux of making bright, new creatures to walk out into the world clothed in flesh. Suddenly I am sitting at the word-processor with two hearts beating inside me.

There is a darker side to the past three years and to the poems. In public places bodies lie on damp concrete, wrapped in blankets and newspapers. Nothing is private – not the shivering nor the open-mouthed sleep nor the need which has to be exposed so that it can be ignored. Bare tattooed flesh on cold November days, shaven heads and pierced faces: these say what can be said with a body and without words except for the ritualised plea for spare change. This is the counterpoint to every trip to town, every humping of groceries into the car boot for the trip home. When I was little and there were no beggars on the streets I read of Victorian children shivering in doorways on Christmas Eve and wondered how anyone could bear to walk past, could refrain from opening their pockets and the doors of their warm houses. Now I know.

TV and radio hammer out a moment-by-moment account of wars we engage in or hold back from. Crackly voices tell of flesh melting in bunkers which the snout of a smart missile has penetrated. I am told of the battle about to start, the one which will transform living bodies to shreds of flesh and will use giant earthmovers to heap sand over them until they are obliterated. We are forced into a conspiracy where we inhabit the same time as sufferings which we pay our taxes to inflict, but cannot alleviate. As we spectate we combine physical immunity with a profound, grievous sense of complicity. In poems such as 'In the Desert Knowing Nothing' and 'Poem on the Obliteration of 100,000 Iraqi Soldiers', I have tried to express this without, I hope, seizing on the sufferings of others in order to demonstrate my own sensitivity.

Mandelstam wrote

> I have the present of a body – what should I do with it
> so unique it is and so much mine?

For me that question raises a hundred others. These poems are ways of finding forms for all these questions, rather than a set of answers.

FROM

Secrets

(1994)

Lemon sole

I lay and heard voices
spin through the house
and there were five minutes to run
for the snow-slewed school bus.

My mother said they had caught it
as she wiped stars from the window –
the frost mended its web
and she put her snow-cool hand to my forehead.

The baby peeked round her skirts
trying to make me laugh
but I said my head hurt
and shut my eyes on her and coughed.

My mother kneeled
until her shape hid the whole world.
She buffed up my pillows as she held me.
'Could you eat a lemon sole?' she asked me.

It was her favourite
she would buy it as a treat for us.
I only liked the sound of it
slim, holy and expensive

but I said 'Yes, I will eat it'
and I shut my eyes and sailed out
on the noise of sunlight, white sheets
and lemon sole softly being cut up.

Christmas caves

A draught like a bony finger
felt under the door

but my father swung the coal scuttle
till the red cave of the fire roared

and the pine-spiced Christmas tree
shook out plumage of glass and tinsel.

The radio was on but ignored,
greeting 'Children all around the world'

and our Co-op Christmas turkey
had gone astray in the postal system –

the headless, green-gibletted corpse
revolved in the sorting-room

its leftover flesh
never to be eaten.

Tomorrow's potatoes rolled to the boil
and a chorister sang like a star

glowing by the lonely moon –
but he was not so far,

though it sounded like Bethlehem
and I was alone in the room

with the gold-netted sherry bottle
and wet black walnuts in a jar.

That violet-haired lady

That violet-haired lady, dowager-
humped, giving herself so many
smiles, taut glittering smiles,
smiles that swallow the air in front of her,
smiles that cling to shop-mirrors
and mar their silvering, smiles
like a spider's wrinklework
flagged over wasteland bushes –

she's had so many nips and tucks,
so much mouse-delicate
invisible mending. Her youth
squeaks out of its prison –
the dark red bar of her mouth
opening and closing.
She wants her hair to look black,
pure black, so she strands it with violet,
copperleaf, burgundy, rust –
that violet-haired lady, dowager-
humped, giving herself
so many smiles, keeping the light on.

Whooper swans

They fly
      straight-necked and barely white
       above the bruised stitching of clouds
       above wind and the sound of storms
        above the creak of the tundra
         the howl of weather
          the scatter
           and wolfish gloom
             of sleet icing their wings,

they come

    on their strong-sheathed wings
     looking at nothing
      straight down a freezing current of light,
      they might
       astonish a sleepy pilot
        tunnelling his route above the Arctic,

    his instruments darken and wink
     circling the swans
    and through his dull high window at sunrise
     he sees them
      ski their freezing current of light
       at twenty-seven thousand feet
        past grey-barrelled engines
         spitting out heat
          across the flight of the swans,

and they're gone
      the polar current sleeking them down
      as soon as he sees them.

Snow Queen

Long long I have looked for you,
snowshoeing across the world
across the wild white world

with my heart in my pocket
and my black-greased boots
to keep the cold out,

past cathedrals and pike marshes
I've tracked you,
so long I have looked for you.

In your star-blue palace
I wandered and could not find you
in your winter garden
I picked icicles,

my fingers burned on your gate
of freezing iron
I have the pain
of it yet on my palm,

through clanging branches
and black frost-fall
I dared not call

so I slide above worlds of ice
where the fishes kiss

and the drowned farmer
whips on his cart
through bubbles of glass

and his dogs prance
at the tail-end, frozen
with one leg cocked
and their yellow urine

twined in thickets of ice.
I stamp my boot
and the ice booms.

I have looked so long
I am wild and white
as your creatures, I might
be one of your own.

The cuckoo game

It starts with breaking into the wood
through a wave of chestnut leaves.

I am grey as a spring morning
fat and fuzzy as pussy willow,

all around I feel them simmering
those nests I've laid in,

like burst buds, a hurt place
lined for the young who've gone

unfledged to the ground.
There they splay, half-eaten

and their parents see nothing
but the one that stays.

This is the weather that cuckoos love:
the breaking of buds,

I am grey in the woods, burgling
the body-heat of birds,

riding the surf of chestnut flowers
on spread feathers.

I love the kiss of a carefully-built nest
in my second of pausing –

this is the way we grow
we cuckoos,

if you think cuckoos never come back
we do. We do.

The butcher's daughter

Where have you been, my little daughter
out in the wild weather?

I have met with a sailor, mother,
he has given me five clubs for juggling
and says I must go with him for ever.

Oh no, my treasure
you must come in and stay for ever
for you are the butcher's daughter.

Where have you been, my little daughter
in the winter weather?

I have met a man of war, mother,
he has given me four hoops to dance through
and he says I must love him for ever.

Oh no, my treasure
you must come in and shut the door
for you are the butcher's daughter.

Where have you been, my little daughter,
out in stormy weather?

I have met with a prince, mother,
he has given me three promises
and I must rule his heart for ever.

Oh no, my treasure
you must give back his promises
for you are the butcher's daughter.

Where have you been, my little daughter
in the wild of the weather?

I have spoken to a wise man, mother,
who gave me knowledge of good and evil
and said I must learn from him for ever.

Oh no, my treasure
you have no need of his knowledge
for you are the butcher's daughter.

Where have you been, my little, daughter
out in the summer weather?

I have met with a butcher, mother,
and he is sharpening a knife for me
for I am the butcher's daughter.

The greenfield ghost

The greenfield ghost is not much of a ghost,
it is a ghost of dammed-up streams,
it is a ghost of slow walks home
and sunburn and blackberry stains.

The greenfield ghost is not much of a ghost.
It is the ghost of low-grade land,
it is the ghost of lovers holding hands
on evening strolls out of town.

The greenfield ghost is not much of a ghost.
It is the ghost of mothers at dusk calling,
it is the ghost of children leaving their dens
for safe houses which will cover them.

Herring girl

See this 'un here, this little bone needle,
he belonged to the net menders.

I heard the crackle in your throat
like fishbone caught there, not words.

And this other 'un, he's wood, look,
you said to the radio interviewer

and I couldn't see the fine-fashioned needle
or the seams on your face,

but I heard the enormous hiss of herring
when they let the tailboard down

and the buyers bargaining
as the tide reached their boots,

I heard the heave of the cart, the herring girls'
laugh as they flashed their knives –

Such lovely voices we all had
you ought t' have heard us
singing like Gracie Fields
or else out of the hymn book.

Up to your elbows, you gutted
your pile of herring. The sludge

was silver, got everywhere.
Your hands were fiery and blooded.

from the slash and the tweak and the salt
and the heap of innards for the gulls.

I'd put a little bit o' bandage round these fingers
– you can see where they been nicked,

we had to keep going so quick
we could never wear gloves.

Russian doll

When I held you up to my cheek you were cold
when I came close to your smile it dissolved,

the paint on your lips was as deep
as the steaming ruby of beetroot soup

but your breath smelled of varnish and pine
and your eyes swivelled away from mine.

When I wanted to open you up
you glowed, dumpy and perfect

smoothing your dozen little selves
like rolls of fat under your apron

and I hadn't the heart to look at them.
I knew I would be spoiling something.

But when I listened to your heart
I heard the worlds inside of you spinning
like the earth on its axis spinning.

Breeze of ghosts

Tall ship hanging out at the horizon
tall ship blistering the horizon
you've been there so long
your sheets and decks white
in the sun

what wind whispers you in?

Tall ship creaking at the horizon
your captain long gone
your crew in the cabin
drinking white rum
their breath spiralling

what wind breathes you in?

Tall ship tilting to the shoreline
past Spanish palms
tall ship coming in like a swan
in the midday sun

what wind blows you in?

It is the cool
wind of the morning
stirring my masts
before the sun
burns it to nothing,
they call it
breeze of ghosts.

FROM

Short Days
Long Nights

(1991)

For my family

Those shady girls

Those shady girls on the green side of the street,
those far-from-green girls who keep to the shade,
those shady girls in mysterious suits
with their labels half-showing
as the cream flap of the jacket swings open,
those girls kicking aside the front-panelled pleats
of their cream suits with cerise lapels,

those on-coming girls,
those girls swinging pearly umbrellas
as tightly-sheathed as tulips in bud
from an unscrupulous street-seller,
those girls in cream and cerise suits
which mark if you touch them,
those girls with their one-name appointments
who walk out of the sunshine.

The dream-life of priests

Do they wake careless and warm
with light on the unwashed windows
and a perpetual smell of bacon,

do their hearts sink at today's martyr
with his unpronounceable name
and strange manner of execution?

Do they wake out of the darkness
with hearts thudding like ours
and reach for the souvenir lamp-switch

then shove a chair against the door
and key facts into the desk-top computer
while cold rattles along the corridor?

Do they cry out in sleep
at some barely-crushed thought,
some failure to see the joke,

or do they rest in their dreams
along the surface of the water
like a bevy of dragonflies

slack and blue in the shallows
whirring among reed-mace and water-forget-me-not
while the ripples cluck?

Do they wake in ordinary time
to green curtains slapping the frame
of a day that'll cloud later on,

to cars nudging and growling for space,
to a baptismal mother, wan with her eagerness
and her sleepless, milk-sodden nights?

Do they reach and stroke the uneven plaster
and sniff the lime-blossom threading
like silk through the room,

or do they wait, stretched out like babies
in the gold of its being too early
with sun on their ceilings wobbling like jelly

while their housekeepers jingle the milk-bottles
and cry 'Father!' in sixty-year-old voices
and scorch toast with devotion –

do they sense the milk in the pan rising
then dive with their blue chins, blundering
through prayer under their honeycomb blankets?

Sisters leaving before the dance

Sisters leaving before the dance,
before the caller gets drunk
or the yellow streamers unreel
looping like ribbons
here and there on the hair of the dancers,

sisters at the turn of the stairs
as the sound system
one-twos, as the squeezebox
mewed in its case

is slapped into breath, and that scrape
of the tables shoved back for the dance
burns like the strike of a match
in the cup of two hands.
Ripe melons and meat

mix in the binbags with cake
puddled in cherry-slime, wind
heavy with tar
blows back the yard door, and I'm

caught with three drinks in my hands
on the stairs looking up
at the sisters leaving before the dance,
not wishing to push past them
in their white broderie anglaise and hemmed

skirts civilly drawn
to their sides to make room
for the big men in suits,
and the girls in cerise

dance-slippers and cross-backed dresses
who lead the way up
and take charge of the tickets, and yet
from their lips cantaloupe
fans as they speak

in bright quick murmurs between
a violin ghosting a tune
and the kids in the bar downstairs
begging for Coke, peaky but certain.

The sisters say their *good nights*
and all the while people stay bunched
on the stairs going up, showing respect
for the small words of the ones leaving,
the ones who don't stay for the dancing.

One sister twists a white candle
waxed in a nest of hydrangeas –
brick-red and uncommon, flowers
she really can't want – she bruises the limp

warm petals with crisp fingers
and then poises her sandal
over the next non-slip stair
so the dance streams at her heels
in the light of a half-shut door.

On not writing certain poems

You put your hand over mine and whispered
'There he is, laying against the pebbles' –
you wouldn't point for the shadow
stirring the trout off his bed
where he sculled the down-running water,

and the fish lay there, unbruised
by the soft knuckling of the river-bed
or your stare which had found him out.

Last night I seemed to be walking
with something in my hand, earthward, down-
dropping as lead, unburnished –

a plate perhaps or a salver
with nothing on it or offered
but its own shineless composure.

I have it here on my palm, the weight
settled, spreading through bone
until my wrist tips backward, pulled down

as if my arm was laid in a current
of eel-dark water – that thrum
binding the fingers – arrow-like –

Privacy of rain

Rain. A plump splash
on tense, bare skin.
Rain. All the May leaves
run upward, shaking.

Rain. A first touch
at the nape of the neck.
Sharp drops kick the dust, white
downpours shudder
like curtains, rinsing
tight hairdos to innocence.

I love the privacy of rain,
the way it makes things happen
on verandahs, under canopies
or in the shelter of trees
as a door slams and a girl runs out
into the black-wet leaves.
By the brick wall an iris
sucks up the rain
like intricate food, its tongue
sherbetty, furred.

Rain. All the May leaves
run upward, shaking.
On the street bud-silt
covers the windscreens.

Dancing man

That lake lies along the shore
like a finger down my cheek,

its waters lull and collapse
dark as pomegranates,

the baby crawls on the straw
in the shadow-map of his father's chair

while the priest talks things over
and light dodges across his hair.

There's a lamp lit in the shed
and a fire on, and a man drinking

spiritus fortis he's made for himself.
But on the floor of the barn

the dancing man is beginning to dance.
First a beat from the arch of his foot

as he stands upright, a neat
understatement of all that's in him

and he lowers his eyes to her
as if it's nothing, nothing –

but she has always wanted him.
Her baby crawls out from the chairs

and rolls in his striped vest laughing
under the feet of the dancers

so she must dance over him
toe to his cheek, heel to his hair,

as she melts to the man dancing.
They are talking and talking over there –

the priest sits with his back to her
for there's no malice in him

and her husband glistens like the sun
through the cypress-flame of the man dancing

In the shed a blackbird
has left three eggs which might be kumquats –

they are so warm. One of them's stirring –
who said she had deserted them?

In the orchard by the barn
there are three girls wading,

glossy, laughing at something,
they spin a bucket between them,

glowing, they are forgotten –
something else is about to happen.

At Cabourg II

The bathers, where are they? The sea is quite empty,
lapsed from its task of rinsing the white beach.

The promenade has a skein of walkers, four to the mile,
like beads threaded on the long Boulevard in front of the flowers.

Shutters are all back on the bankers' fantasy houses,
but the air inside is glassy as swimming-pool water,

no one breathes there or silts it with movement,
Out of the kitchen a take-away steam rises:

the bankers are having sushi in honour of their guests
who are here, briefly, to buy 'an impressionist picture'.

A boy is buried up to his neck in sand
but the youth leader stops another who pretends to piss on him.

The rest draw round, they have got something helpless:
his head laid back on its platter of curls.

With six digging, he's out in a minute.
They oil his body with Ambre Solaire,

two boys lay him across their laps, a third
wipes at his feet then smiles up enchantingly.

Baron Hardup

I see the boys at the breakwater
straighten now, signalling friends,
and the little imperious one who is just not
dinted at the back of the arms
with child-like softness
sticks up his thumb to mark the next leap.

This far off it's peaceful to watch them
while I'm walking ahead barefoot
on a wide, grey Norman promenade,
thinking of the Baron de Charlus
not in his wheelchair but younger,
bumbling into seduction in a hot courtyard,

tipped upside-down like a sand-timer,
labelled implacably – 'the invert'
caught at the wide-striped
dawn years of the century
where the candy of skirts blows inward and outward
to a pure, bellying offshore wind.

The beautiful line of his coat ripples –
he's Baron Hardup with dreams tupping
like pantomime horses – he fixes his eyeglass
and glares at the waves with passionate indecisiveness
as if to stop, or not stop, their irregular fall,
while the boys figure what he is good for.

Nearly May Day

After a night jagged by guard-dogs and nightingales
I sit to be videoed
at the corner of this carved balcony
where ten o'clock sun falls
past the curve of the Berlin Wall.
It's nearly May Day.
Just here there's a double wall –
a skin of concrete, a skin of stone
the colour of the Alsatians.

My feet shift on the slats.
I want to comb my hair straight.
I have my back
to a wood in the closed zone –
an orchard's bright pelt
sparkling with blossom tips.
Bees fly in purposeful zigzags
over the Wall, tracing their map
of air and nectar.
Each day they fly through the spoors
of air-wiping floodlights now
sheathed in the watch-towers
to this one apple tree
which makes a garden of itself
under the balcony.

I have my back to the church.
Its roof glows in the gaps
where slate after slate's peeled off.
I have my back to the porch
with its red lining of valerian,
its sound like a cough
as the doors squeeze themselves shut.
Katja unrolls cable
over the balcony rail.
A double wiring of roses
straddles the pews
in a hamlet which is the other half of here,
clear and suggestive as a mirror.

They say nobody lives there
but guards' wives and children.
You rarely see them,
they melt into the woods like foxes
but you hear their motorbikes miles off
clutching the road surface.
You might hear the guards' wives say
'Let the kids have the grapes'
just as the nightingales insist
for hours when you can't sleep.

This hamlet's like something I've dreamed
in a dream broken by rain,
with its lilac and dull green
tenderly shifting leaves,
its woodpiles,
its watched inhabitants,
wives of the guards
who have between them a little son
in a too-tight yellow jersey
flashing along their own balcony.

He runs from his steep-roofed home
to scrabble onto his tricycle
and race with fat frantic legs pedalling
the few square metres marked by the wives
with a shield-square of clothes-line
where they're forever hanging things out
while my back's turned.
I study the guards' underpants
and wish I still smoked
so I could blow smoke-rings
from the balcony of Jagdschloss Glienicke
past the flowering jaws of the apple tree
over complicated roof-shells
to the child himself.
I'd wave, holding the cigarette
cupped behind my back.

Any time they choose
people are changing Deutschmarks
for a tick on cheap paper,
a day-trip to the East
to buy Bulgarian church music
and butter at half-price,
to check their faces in a mirror
and get it all on video.
to walk through a map of mirrors
into the other half of here.

There's mist on the Glienicke bridge.
The flags are limp.
There's nothing flying at all –
not a flag, not an aeroplane
racing down safe corridors.

It's nearly May Day.
A riot's ripening in Kreuzberg.
If this is Spring, it's going on elsewhere
grasping horse-chestnut buds
in sticky hands
warm and forgetful
as a child who buries himself
for joy in Pankow's warm sands.

[September 1989]

Three workmen with blue pails

Three workmen with blue pails
swerve past an election poster
wrapped round a lamp-post pillar,

signed with a single carnation
and a name for each ward.
The workmen guffaw –

it's five past three on a small street
which traipses off Unter den Linden
deep into East Berlin.

Short, compact and bored
they tramp over the slats
where the pavement's torn up.

One of them's telling a joke.
They swing on under a banner
for a play by Harold Pinter –

stretched linen, four metres wide
and at least two workmen tall,
spread on a ten-metre wall –

the play's *The Dumb Waiter*.
They go on past a kindergarten
which is tipping out children,

past banks with bullet-holes in them,
past an industrial shoal
of tower-block homes

to the second-right turn
where the pulse of street-life picks up,
where there are people and shops.

Ahead, a queue forms
as a café rattles itself open
and starts to serve out ice cream.

Inside his treacle-brown frame
a young man flickers and smiles
as he fans out the biscuit-shells –

already half the ice cream's gone
and the waiter teases the children
with cold smoke from a new can.

Seeds stick to their tongues –
gooseberry, cloudberry – chill,
grainy and natural.

Shoving their caps back
the workmen join on
and move forward in line

for what's over. Tapping light coins
they move at a diagonal
to a blue, skew-whiff ditched Trabbi.

Brown coal

The room creaked like a pair of lungs
and the fire wouldn't go
till we held up the front page for it.
All the while the news was on

that day they wired up the Wall
while I was swimming on newspaper –
a cold rustle of words
to the wheezing of my sister.

I caught the fringe of her scarf
in winter smogs after school
as she towed me through the stutter
of high-lamped Ford Populars

and down the mouth of the railway tunnel
into water-pocked walls
and the dense sulphurous hollows
of nowhere in particular.

It was empty but for smog.
Coughing through our handkerchiefs
we walked eerily, lammed
at the brickwork, picked ourselves up.

I walked through nowhere last April
into a mist of brown coal,
sulphur emissions, diesel
stopped dead at the Wall,

the whiff of dun Trabants
puttering north/south
past a maze of roadworks,
leaving hours for us to cross

in the slow luxury of strolling
as the streets knit themselves up
to become a city again.
By instinct I kept my mouth shut

and breathed like one of us girls
in our "identical-twin" coats,
listening out for rare cars,
coal at the back of our throats –

it was England in the fifties,
half-blind with keeping us warm,
so I was completely at ease
in a small street off Unter Den Linden

as a fire-door behind wheezed
and Berlin creaked like two lungs.

Safe period

Your dry voice from the centre of the bed
asks 'Is it safe?'

and I answer for the days as if I owned them.
Practised at counting, I rock
the two halves of the month like a cradle.

The days slip over their stile
and expect nothing. They are just days,

and we're at it again, thwarting
souls from the bodies they crave.

They'd love to get into this room
under the yellow counterpane
we've torn to make a child's cuddly,

they'd love to slide into the sheets
between soft, much-washed
flannelette fleece,

they'd love to be here in the moulded spaces
between us, where there is no room,

but we don't let them. They fly about gustily,
noisy as our own children.

Big barbershop man

Big barbershop man turning away,
sides of his face
lathered and shaved
close with the cut-throat
he always uses,

big barbershop man turning away,
helping the neighbours
make good, sweating
inside a stretched t-shirt
with NO MEANS YES on the back of it,

waltzing a side of pig,
taking the weight,
scalp like a glove
rucked with the strain,
big barbershop man turning away
trim inside like a slice of ham

big barbershop man
hoisting the forequarter,
fat marbled with meat
stiff as a wardrobe,

big barbershop man
waltzing a side of pig
striped like a piece
of sun awning, cool
as a jelly roll,
big barbershop man waltzing the meat
like a barber's pole on yellow Main Street.

The dry well

It was not always a dry well.
Once it had been brimming with water.
cool, limpid, delicious water,
but a man came and took water from the well
and a woman came and took water from the well
and a man took water from the well again

       and the well could not drink
       from the low, slack water-table.

The well lacked a sense of its own danger
and a man came to take water from the well
and a woman came to take water from the well

       but as the man was coming again
       the well sighed in the dry darkness,
       the well spoke in a quiet voice
       from the deep-down bell of its emptiness
       Give me some water.

But the man was at work with his heavy bucket
and he cried cheerfully, *Wait half a minute,*
I will just draw one more bucketful!

When he swung it up it was full of dust
and he was angry with the well.
Could it not have held out longer?
He had only needed one more bucketful.

Our family, swimming again

Our family, swimming again.
Slick lily-ropes, flat as gelled hair,
pull under the surface.
The four lads with an army feel to them
grin and are gone
leaving the splash of their voices
like a high-water-mark, drying
on the concrete landing-stage
where we splay and bake in the sun.

My husband says he's standing on sand
and can touch its clean ribs with his feet,
but I hang, vertical,
sleeved with the cold, my mouth level
with the smooth purl of the current
like yards of candy being pulled,
while in a hospital core
sticky as the inside of wedding-cake,
snail-vaulted ear-walls
fill up with electricity.

This current's for hauling us off
by the hair, making it flow upright.
Yes, but I might
yet side-slip or trick it.
For all the cover my clothes give
I may as well swim naked.

A physiotherapist sighs with the heat
as she bends, unplaiting the tendons
healed wrong in my father's feet.
He hears her dap off down the corridor
then feels in his right-hand drawer
and works away with the polish I gave him
to make a mid-tan gloss on his sandals.
There's a quick, willowy landscape in yellows
done by the Sinhalese charge-nurse –

but this is not a poem about him.
I like the look of what it's not.
For a moment out of reach
in my bra with its lace half-off
I'm just swimming unexpectedly
under the vaults of the aqueduct,
kicking free of the lilies
which thrust bare buds inches above me.

My husband calls me to stop.
I tip on my back and stare up
the vaults' inner greased walls.
There's a man watching me swim,
one big hand clamped to the parapet,
the other combing for sounds on his Walkman.

Sweet pepper

See, you have fallen asleep in spite of me
and my heels going and returning,
with your blankets tucked and your hard-eyed toy dog
wedged under your arm.

In your dream two children are climbing a summer mountain.
They pass the snake-pit, tangled and blue
with smoke of sliding yellow and black snakes –

these will not hurt you. Your brother and Becky
branch like skaters from path fork to path
and so upwards and gone, with the thin girl

driving ahead, and the slower
graceful, compact boy stopped, lingering
over a stand of flowerless balsam.

See, you throw out your hand to the wall
where the children are crying and laughing
after their day lost on the mountain –
but here the sky sweats with excess of rain,

you're far away from yourself, and I'm
unjamming the window to night air
soaked through with the storm, bruised
fresh as a sweet pepper.

Heron

It's evening on the river,
steady, milk-warm,

the nettles head-down
with feasting caterpillars,

the current turning,
thin as a blade-bone.

Reed-mace shivers.
I'm miles from anywhere.

Who's looking?
did a fish jump?

– and then a heron goes up
from its place by the willow.

With ballooning flight
it picks up the sky

and makes off, loaded.
I wasn't looking,

I heard the noise of its wings
and I turned,

I thought of a friend,
a cool one with binoculars,

here's rarity
with big wing-flaps, suiting itself.

One yellow chicken

One yellow chicken
she picks up expertly and not untenderly
from the conveyor of chickens.

Its soft beak gobbles feverishly
at a clear liquid which might be
a dose of sugar-drenched serum –

the beak's flexible membrane
seems to engulf the chicken
as it tries to fix on the dropper's glass tip.

Clear yellow juice gulps through a tube
and a few drops, suddenly colourless,
swill round a gape wide as the brim of a glass

but the chicken doesn't seem afraid –
or only this much, only for this long
until the lab assistant flicks it back on
to the slowly moving conveyor of chickens
and it tumbles, catches itself,
then buoyed up by the rest
reels out of sight, cheeping.

Sailing to Cuba

I'd climbed the crab-apple in the wind
that wild season of Cuba,

I leaned out on the twigs
to where clouds heeled over like sails
on the house-bounded horizon,

but even from here I felt the radio throb
like someone who was there when the accident happened
'not two yards from where I was standing',

then Big Band music cha-cha'd from room to room
to fill in time between news.

At school we learned 'Quinquireme of Nineveh
from distant Ophir...' The ships nudged closer.
The wind roared to itself like applause.

Off the West Pier

Dropped yolks of shore-lamp quiver on tarmac –
the night's disturbed and the sea itself
sidles about after its storm, buttery,
melting along the groynes.

The sea's a martinet with itself,
will come this far and no farther
like a Prussian governess
corrupted by white sugar –

Oh but the stealth
with which it twitches aside mortar
and licks, and licks
moist grains off the shore.

By day it simply keeps marching
beat after beat like waves of soldiers
timed to the first push. In step with the music
it swells greenness and greyness, spills foam
onto a fly-swarming tide-line –
beertabs and dropped King Cones,
flotsam of inopportune partners
sticky with what came after.

A man lies on his back
settled along the swell, his knees
glimmering, catching a lick of moonlight,
lazy as a seagull on Christmas morning –
He should have greased himself with whale-blubber
like a twelve-year-old Goddess-chested
cross-Channel swimmer.
His sadness stripes through him like ink
leaving no space or him.
He paws slow arm sweeps and rolls
where the sea shoulders him.

Up there an aeroplane falters,
its red landing-lights on
scouting the coast home.
The pilot smokes a cigarette.
Its tip winks with each breath.

Winter 1955

We're strung out on the plain's upthrust,
bubbles against the sill of the horizon.
Already the dark folds each figure to itself
like a mother putting on her child's overcoat,
or a paid attendant, who quickly and deftly
slots goose-pimpled arms into their stoles.

My own mother is attending to her daughters
in the Christmas gloom of our long garden
before the others are born.
A stream's tongue takes its first courses:
in siren suits and our cheek-hugging bonnets
we put one foot each in that water.

Now standstill clumps sink and disappear
over the plate-edge of the world.
The trees hold up fingers like candelabra,
blue and unsure as the word 'distant'.
Casually heeled there, we circle
the New Look skirts of our mother.

The attendant's hands skim on a breast
fused into party-going ramparts of taffeta,
but he takes up his gaze into the hall
as if there's nothing to be sorry or glad for,
and nothing in the snowy eternity
that feathers his keyhole.

Rinsing

In the corded hollows of the wood
leaves fall.
How light it is.
The trees are rinsing themselves of leaves
like Degas laundresses, their forearms
cold with the jelly-smooth
blue of starch-water.

The laundresses lean back and yawn
with their arms still in the water
like beech-boughs, pliant
on leavings of air.

In the corded hollows of the wood
how light it is.
How my excitement
burns in the chamber.

To Betty, swimming

You're breast-up in the bubbling spaces you make for yourself,
your head in the air, pointy, demure,
ridiculous in its petalled swim-cap.

You chug slowly across the pool.
Your legs trail. Your arms won't sweep
more than a third of the full stroke,

yet when you look up you're curling with smiles,
complicit as if splashed
with mile-deep dives from the cliff's height.

In Berber's Ice Cream Parlour

A fat young man in BERBER'S ICE CREAM PARLOUR
under a tiled ceiling the colour of farm butter
with a mirror at 45° to his jaw.

His moist jowls, lucent and young
as the tuck where a baby's buttock and thigh join,
quiver a little, preparing
to meet the order he's given.

A tall glass skims the waitress's breasts.
He holds on, spoon poised
to see if the syrup'll trickle right

past the mound of chopped nuts to the ice-
white luscious vanilla sheltering
under its blanket of cream.

The yellow skin weakens and melts.
He devotes himself,
purses his lips to wrinkling-point,

digs down with the long spoon
past jelly and fruit
to the depths, with the cool
inching of an expert.

Beside him there's a landscape in drained pink
and blue suggesting the sea
with an audacious cartoon economy.
They've even put in one white triangle
to make the horizon. A sail.

Large creamy girls mark the banana splits
with curls and squiggles,
pour sauce on peach melbas,
thumb in real strawberries.

Their bodies sail behind the counters,
balloons tight at the ropes, held down
by a customer's need for more clotted cream
topping on his three-tier chocolate sundae.

They have eight tables to serve.
With their left hands they slap out the change
and comets smelling of nickel
for kids' take-away treats,

and over on the bar counter there's room
for adult, luxurious absorption
of dark mocha ice cream.

Flowing, damp-curled, the waitresses
pass with their trays
doubled by mirrors, bumping like clouds.

On drinking lime juice in September

(for Patrick Charnley)

How the sick body calms itself
and knows it is blissful to live.
The lime juice of long voyages
fans through each tissue.

Ultramarine stands at the masts,
the long wake purls, barbarous sailors
wait round the canvas, heads bowed.

The captain, your ancestor,
fell from the grace of his life one voyage
west from Australia. They made him
his shroud of sailcloth with quick stitches.

They stole his book of the burial service
out of his pocket: now it was theirs
to read through slowly, becalmed,
in its long, sea-remembering cadences.

They launched his vessel of flesh
where it would dive, darken,
cast up its sewn air,
its gene code with a hundred answers.

Not going to the forest

If you had said the words 'to the forest'
at once I would have gone there
leaving my garden of broccoli and potato-plants.

I would not have struggled

to see the last ribbons of daylight
and windy sky tear over the crowns
of the oaks which stand here,
heavy draught animals
bearing, continually bearing.

I would have rubbed the velvety forest
against my cheek like the pincushion
I sewed with invisible stitches.

No. But you said nothing
and I have a child to think of
and a garden of parsnips and raspberries.
It's not that I'm afraid,
but that I'm still gathering
the echoes of my five senses –

how far they've come with me, how far
they want to go on.

So the whale-back of the forest
shows for an instant, then dives.
I think it has oxygen within it
to live, downward, for miles.

Lutherans

Whichever way I turned on the radio
there was Sibelius
or an exceptionally long weather forecast.
Good practice: I'd purse up my lips
to the brief gulp of each phrase.

Sometimes I struck a chord with the World Service's
sense-fuzz, like the smell of gardenia
perfume in Woolworth's: instantly cloying,
the kind that doesn't bloom on your skin,

or, in the two P.M. gloom of the town square,
I'd catch the pale flap of a poster
for the Helsingin Sanomat: POMPIDOU KUOLLUT.
I'd buy one, but never wrestle beyond the headline.

When pupils asked what I thought of 'this three-day week'
I'd mention the candle-blaze
nightly in my room during the power-cuts,
and the bronchitis I had,
but I'd balance the fact that I smoked too much
against the marsh-chill when the heating went off.

I'd always stop on the railway bridge
even at one in the morning. The city was shapeless, squeezed in
by hills bristling with Sitka spruce.
The drunks had their fires lit
but they were slow, vulnerable, frozen
while flaming on a half-litre from the State Alcohol Shop.

If their luck held they'd bunch on the Sports Hall heating-grates
rather than be chipped free from a snow heap
in the first light of ten in the morning,
among a confusion of fur-hatted burghers
going to have coffee and cakes.
Work started at eight, there was never enough time.
They'd stop, chagrined, and murmur 'It's shocking'.

They were slowly learning not to buy the full-cream milk
of their farming childhoods; there was a government campaign
with leaflets on heart disease and exercise
and a broadsheet on the energy crisis
with diagrams suggesting the angles
beyond which windows should never be opened.

Their young might be trim, but they kept
a pious weakness for sinning on cake
and for those cloudy, strokeable hats
that frame Lutheran pallor.
After an evening visit to gym, they'd roll
the green cocoon of their ski-suited baby
onto the pupils' table. Steadied with one hand
it lay prone and was never unpacked.

The Raw Garden

(1988)

To Mike Levine and David Stewart

Code-breaking in the Garden of Eden

The Raw Garden is a collection of closely related poems, which are intended to speak to, through, and even over each other. The poems draw their full effect from their setting; they feed from each other, even when the link is as mild as an echo of phrasing or cadence.

It is now possible to insert new genes into a chromosomal pattern. It is possible to feed in new genetic material, or to remove what is seen as faulty or damaged material. The basic genetic code is contained in DNA (deoxyribonucleic acid), and its molecular structure is the famous double helix, so called because it consists of two complementary spirals which match each other like the halves of a zip. Naturally occurring enzymes can be used to split the double strand, and to insert new material. The separate strands are then recombined to form the complete DNA helix. By this process of gene-splicing a new piece of genetic information can be inserted into a living organism, and can be transmitted to the descendants of the organism.

It seems to me that there is an echo of this new and revolutionary scientific process in the way each poet feeds from the material drawn together in a long poetic tradition, "breaks" it with his or her individual creative voice, and re-combines it through new poems.

One thing I have tried to do in these poems is to explore the effect which these new possibilities of genetic manipulation may have on our concept of what is natural and what is unnatural. If we can not follow Romantic poets in their assumption of a massive, unmalleable landscape which moulds the human creatures living upon it and provides them with a constant, stable frame of reference, then how do we look at landscape and at the "natural"? We are used to living in a profoundly human-made landscape. As I grew up I realised that even such apparently wild places as moors and commons were the product of human decisions and work: people had cut down trees, grazed animals, acquired legal rights. But still this knowledge did not interfere with my sense that these places were natural.

The question might be, what does it take to disturb the sense of naturalness held by the human being in his or her, landscape? Is there a threshold beyond which a person revolts at a feeling that changedness has gone too far? Many of these poems focus on highly manipulated landscapes and outcrops of "nature", and on the harmonies and revulsions formed between them and the people living among them.

Perhaps the Garden of Eden embodies some yearning to print down an idea of the static and the predictable over our knowledge that we have to accept perpetual changeability. The code of the Garden of Eden has been broken open an infinite number of times. Now we are faced with a still greater potential for change, since we have acquired knowledge of the double helix structure of DNA. If the Garden of Eden really exists it does so moment by moment, fragmented and tough, cropping up like a fan of buddleia high up in the gutter of a deserted warehouse, or in a heap of frozen cabbages becoming luminous in the reflected light off roadside snow. This Garden of Eden propagates itself in strange ways, some of which find parallels in far-fetched horticultural techniques such as air layering, or growing potatoes in a mulch of rotted seaweed on white sand. I hope that these poems do not seem to hanker back to a prelapsarian state of grace. If I want to celebrate anything, it is resilience, adaptability, and the power of improvisation.

Seal run

The potatoes come out of the earth bright
as if waxed, shucking their compost,

and bob against the palm of my hand
like the blunt muzzles of seals swimming.

Slippy and pale in the washing-up bowl
they bask, playful, grown plump
in banks of seaweed on white sand,

seaweed hauled from brown circles
set in transparent waters off Easdale

all through the sun-fanned West Highland midnights
when the little potatoes are seeding there
to make necklaces under the mulch,
torques and amulets in their burial place.

The seals quiver, backstroking
for pure joy of it, down to the tidal
slim mouth of the loch,

they draw their lips back, their blunt whiskers
tingle at the inspout of salt water

then broaching the current they roll
off between islands and circles of oarweed.

At noon the sea-farmer
turns back his blanket of weed
and picks up potatoes like eggs
from their fly-swarming nest,

too fine for the sacks, so he puts them in boxes
and once there they smell earthy.

At noon the seals nose up the rocks
to pile there, sun-dazed,
back against belly, island on island.

and sleep, shivering like dogs
against the tug of the stream
flowing on south past Campbelltown.

The man's hands rummage about still
to find what is full-grown there.
Masts on the opposite shore ring faintly

disturbing themselves, and make him look up.
Hands down and still moving
he works on, his fingers at play blinded,
his gaze roving the ripe sea-loch.

Wild strawberries

What I get I bring home to you:
a dark handful, sweet-edged,
dissolving in one mouthful.

I bother to bring them for you
though they're so quickly over,
pulpless, sliding to juice,

a grainy rub on the tongue
and the taste's gone. If you remember
we were in the woods at wild strawberry time

and I was making a basket of dockleaves
to hold what you'd picked,
but the cold leaves unplaited themselves

and slid apart, and again unplaited themselves
until I gave up and ate wild strawberries
out of your hands for sweetness.

I lipped at your palm –
the little salt edge there,
the tang of money you'd handled.

As we stayed in the wood, hidden,
we heard the sound system below us
calling the winners at Chepstow,
faint as the breeze turned.

The sun came out on us, the shade blotches
went hazel: we heard names
bubble like stock-doves over the woods

as jockeys in stained silks gentled
those sweat-dark, shuddering horses
down to the walk.

A mortgage on a pear tree

A pear tree stands in its own maze.
It does not close its blossom all night
but holds out branchfuls of cool
wide-open flowers. Its slim leaves look black
and stir like tongues in the lamp-light.

It was here before the houses were built.
The owner grew wasteland and waited for values to rise.
The builders swerved a boundary sideways
to cup the tree in a garden. When they piled rubble
it was a soft cairn mounting the bole.

The first owner of the raw garden
came out and walked on the clay clods.
There was the pear tree, bent down
with small blunt fruits, each wide where the flower was,
shaped like a medlar, but sweet.

The ground was dense with fermenting pears,
half trodden to pulp, half eaten.
She could not walk without slipping.

Slowly she walked in her own maze,
sleepy, feeling the blood seep
down her cold fingers, down the spread branch
of veins which trails to the heart,

and remembered how she'd stood under a tree
holding out arms, with two school-friends.
It was the fainting-game,
played in the dinner-hour from pure boredom,
never recalled since. For years this was growing
to meet her, and now she's signed for her own
long mortgage over the pear tree
and is the gainer of its accrued beauty,

but when she goes into her bedroom
and draws her curtains against a spring night
the pear tree does not close its white blossom.
The flowers stay open with slim leaves flickering around them:
touched and used, they bear fruit.

A pæony truss on Sussex Place

Restless, the pæony truss tosses about
in a destructive spring wind.
Already its inner petals are white
without one moment of sun-warmed expansion.

The whole bunch of the thing looks poor
as a stout bare-legged woman in November
slopping her mules over the post office step
to cash a slip of her order book.

The wind rips round the announced site
for inner city conversion: this is the last tough
bit of the garden, with one lilac
half sheared-off and half blooming.

The AIDS ad is defaced and the Australian
lager-bright billboard smirks down
on wind-shrivelled passersby who stayed put
to vote in the third Thatcher election.

The porch of the Elim Pentecostal Church brightens
as a woman in crimson and white suit
steps out, pins her hat down
then grasps the hands of her wind-tugged grandchildren.

Permafrost

For all frozen things –
my middle finger that whitens
from its old, ten-minute frostbite,

for black, slimy potatoes
left in the clamp,
for darkness and cold like cloths
over the cage,

for permafrost, lichen crusts
nuzzled by reindeer,
the tender balance of decades
null as a vault.

For all frozen things –
the princess and princes
staring out of their bunker
at the original wind,

for NATO survivors in nuclear moonsuits
whirled from continent to continent

like Okies in bumpy Fords
fleeing the dustbowl.

For all frozen things –
snowdrops and Christmas roses
blasted down to the germ
of their genetic zip-code.

They fly by memory –
cargo of endless winter,
clods of celeriac, chipped
turnips, lanterns at ten A.M.

in the gloom of a Finnish market lace;
flowers under glass, herring,
little wizened apples.

For all frozen things –
the nipped fish in a mess of ice,
the uncovered galleon
tossed from four centuries of memory,

or nuclear snowsuits bouncing on dust,
trapped on the rough ride of the earth's surface,
on the rough swing of its axis,

like moon-men lost on the moon
watching the earth's green flush

tremble and perish.

At Cabourg

Later my stepson will uncover a five-inch live shell
from a silted pool on the beach at St Côme. It is complete
with brass cap and a date on it: nineteen forty-three.
We'll look it up in the dictionary, take it
to show at the Musée de la Libération
– ce petit obus – but once they unwrap it
they'll drop the polite questions and scramble
full tilt for the Gendarmerie opposite.
The gendarmes will peer through its cradle of polythene
gingerly, laughing. One's at the phone
already – he gestures – 'Imagine! Let's tell them
we've got a live shell here in the Poste!'

Of course this will have happened before.
They'll have it exploded, there'll be no souvenir shell-case,
and we'll be left with our photographs
taken with a camera which turns out to be broken.

Later we'll be at the Château Fontaine-Henry
watching sleek daughters in jodhpurs come in from the fields.
I'll lie back in my green corduroy coat, and leave,
faint, to drive off through fields of sunflowers
without visiting the rooms we've paid for.
Madame will have her fausse-couche,
her intravenous injections, her glass ampoules,
in a room which is all bed
and smells of medicinal alcohol and fruit.
The children will play on the beach, a little forlornly,
in the wind which gusts up out of nowhere.

Later we'll see our friends on their lightweight bicycles
freewheeling tiredly downhill to Asnelles.
Their little son, propped up behind them
will glide past, silent, though he alone sees us.

But now we are on the beach at Cabourg,
stopped on our walk to look where the sky's whitening
over the sea beyond Dives. Now a child squawks
and races back as a wave slaps over his shorts' hem

to where a tanned woman with naked breasts
fidgets her baby's feet in the foam
straight down from the Boulevard Marcel Proust.

Ploughing the roughlands

It's not the four-wheeled drive crawler
spitting up dew and herbs,

not Dalapon followed by dressings
of dense phosphates,

nor ryegrass greening behind wire as behind glass,

not labourers wading in moonsuits
through mud gelded by paraquat –

but now, the sun-yellow, sky-blue
vehicles mount the pale chalk,

the sky bowls on the white hoops
and white breast of the roughland,

the farmer with Dutch eyes
guides forward the quick plough.

Now, flush after flush of Italian ryegrass
furs up the roughland

with its attentive, bright,
levelled-off growth –

pale monoculture
sweating off rivers of filth

fenced by the primary
colours of crawler and silo.

The land pensions

The land pensions, like rockets
shoot off from wheat with a soft yellow
flame-bulb: a rook or a man in black
flaps upwards with white messages.

On international mountains and spot markets
little commas of wheat translate.
The stony ground's pumped to a dense fire
by the flame-throwing of chemicals.
On stony ground the wheat can ignite
its long furls.

The soft rocket of land pensions flies
and is seen in Japan, covering
conical hills with its tender stars:
now it is firework time, remembrance
and melt-down of autumn chrysanthemums.

On bruised fields above Brighton
grey mould laces the wheat harvest.
The little rockets are black. Land pensions
fasten on silos elsewhere, far off.

Market men flicker and skulk like eels
half-way across earth to breed.
On thin chipped flint-and-bone land
a nitrate river laces the grey wheat
pensioning off chalk acres.

A dream of wool

Decoding a night's dreams
of sheepless uplands
the wool-merchant clings to the wool churches,

to trade with the Low Countries,
to profitable, downcast
ladies swathed in wool sleeves

whose plump, light-suffused faces
gaze from the triptychs he worships.

Sheep ticks, maggoty tails and foot-rot
enter his tally of dense beasts, walking
with a winter's weight on their backs

through stubborn pasture
they graze to a hairsbreadth.

From the turf of the Fire Hills
the wool-merchant trawls
sheep for the marsh markets.
They fill mist with their thin cries –

circular eddies, bemusing
the buyers of mutton
from sheep too wretched to fleece.

In the right angle of morning sunshine
the aerial photographer
shoots from the blue,

decodes a landscape
of sheepless uplands
and ploughed drove roads,

decodes the airstream, the lapis lazuli
coat for many compacted skeletons
seaming the chalk by the sea.

New crops

O engines
flying over the light, barren
as shuttles, thrown over a huge
woof

crossply
of hedgeless snail tracks,
you are so high,

you've felled the damp crevices

you've felled the boulder-strewn meadow
the lichen
the strong plum tree.

O engines
swaying your rubber batons
on pods, on ripe lupins,
on a chameleon terrace
of greenlessness,

you're withdrawn from a sea
of harvests, you're the foreshore

of soaked soil leaching
undrinkable streams.

Shadows of my mother against a wall

The wood-pigeon rolls soft notes off its breast
in a tree which grows by a fence.
The smell of creosote,
easy as wild gum
oozing from tree boles
keeps me awake. A thunderstorm
heckles the air.

I step into a bedroom
pungent with child's sleep,
and lift the potty and pile of picture books
so my large shadow
crosses his eyes.

Sometimes at night, expectant,
I think I see the shadow of my mother
bridge a small house of enormous rooms.
Here are white, palpable walls
and stories of my grandmother:
the old hours of tenderness I missed.

Air layering

The rain was falling down in slow pulses
between the horse-chestnuts, as if it would set root there.

It was a slate-grey May evening
luminous with new leaves.
I was at a talk on the appearances of Our Lady
these past five years at Medjugorje.
We sat in a small room in the Presbytery:
the flow of the video scratched, the raindrop
brimmed its meniscus upon the window
from slant runnel to sill.

Later I watched a programme on air layering.
The round rootball steadied itself
high as a chaffinch nest, and then deftly
the gardener severed the new plant.
She knew its wounded stem would have made roots there.

The argument

It was too hot, that was the argument.
I had to walk a mile with my feet flaming
from brown sandals and sun.

Now the draggling shade of the privet made me to dawdle,
now soft tarmac had to be crossed.
I was lugging an old school-bag –

it was so hot the world was agape with it.
One limp rose fell as I passed.

An old witch sat in her front garden
under the spokes of a black umbrella
lashed to her kitchen chair.
God was in my feet as I fled past her.

Everyone I knew was so far away.
The yellow glob of my ice cream melted and spread.
I bought it with huge pennies, held up.
'A big one this time!' the man said,
so I ate on though it cloyed me.
It was for fetching the bread
one endless morning before Bank Holiday.

I was too young, that was the argument,
and had to propitiate everyone:
the man with the stroke, and the burnt lady
whose bared, magical teeth made me
smile if I could –
Oh the cowardice of my childhood!

The peach house

The dry glasshouse is almost empty.
A few pungent geraniums with lost markings
lean in their pots.

It is nothing but a cropping place for sun
on cold Northumbrian July days.

The little girl, fresh from suburbia,
cannot believe in the peaches she finds here.
They are green and furry as monkeys –
she picks them and drops them.

All the same they are matched to the word peach
and must mean more than she sees. She will post them
unripe in a tiny envelope
to her eight-year-old class-mates, and write
carefully in the ruled-up spaces:
'Where we are the place is a palace.'

A meditation on the glasshouses

The bald glasshouses stretch here for miles.
For miles air-vents open like wings.

This is the land of reflections, of heat
flagging from.mirror to mirror. Here cloches
force on the fruit by weeks, while pulses
of light run down the chain of glasshouses
and blind the visitors this Good Friday.

The daffodil pickers are spring-white.
Their neat heads in a fuzz of sun
stoop to the buds, make leafless
bunches of ten for Easter.

A white thumb touches the peat
but makes no print. This is the soil-less
Eden of glasshouses, heat-stunned.

The haunting of Epworth

Epworth Rectory was the childhood home of John Wesley.
In December 1716 the house was possessed by a poltergeist;
after many unsuccessful attempts at exorcism the spirit,
nicknamed 'Old Jeffery' by the little Wesley girls, left
of its own accord.

Old Jeffery begins his night music.
The girls, sheathed in their brick skin,
giggle with terror. The boys are all gone
out to the world, 'continually sinning',
their graces exotic and paid for.

Old Jeffery rummages pitchforks
up the back chimney. The girls
open the doors to troops of exorcists
who plod back over the Isle of Axeholme
balked by the house. The scrimmage
of iron, shattering windows, and brickwork
chipped away daily is birdsong
morning and evening, or sunlight
into their unsunned lives.

Old Jeffery tires of the house slowly.
He knocks the back of the connubial bed
where nineteen Wesleys, engendered in artlessness
swarm, little ghosts of themselves.
The girls learn to whistle his music.

The house bangs like a side-drum
as Old Jeffery goes out of it. Daughters
in white wrappers mount to the windows, sons
coming from school make notes – the wildness
goes out towards Epworth and leaves nothing
but the bald house straining on tiptoe
after its ghost.

Preaching at Gwennap

Gwennap Pit is a natural amphitheatre
in Cornwall, where John Wesley preached.

Preaching at Gwennap, silk
ribbons unrolling far off,
the unteachable turquoise and green
coast dropping far off,

preaching at Gwennap, where thermals revolve
to the bare lip, where granite
breaks its uneasy backbone,
where a great natural theatre, cut
to a hairsbreadth, sends back each cadence,

preaching at Gwennap to a child asleep
while the wide plain murmurs, and prayers
ply on the void, tendered like cords
over the pit's brim.
                            Off to one side
a horse itches and dreams. Its saddle
comes open, stitch after stitch,

while the tired horse, standing for hours
flicks flies from its arse
and eats through the transfiguration –
old sobersides
mildly eschewing more light.

On circuit from Heptonstall Chapel

Tis not everyone could bear these things, but I bless God,
my wife is less concerned with suffering them than
I in writing them.'

SAMUEL WESLEY, father of John Wesley,
writing of his wife Susanna

The mare with her short legs heavily mud-caked
plods, her head down
over the unearthly grasses,
the burning salt-marshes,

through sharp-sided marram and mace
with the rim of the tide's eyelid
out to the right.

The reed-cutters go home
whistling sharply, crab-wise
beneath their dense burdens,

the man on the mare weighs heavy, his broadcloth
shiny and wom, his boots dangling
six inches from ground.
He clenches his buttocks to ease them,
shifts Bible and meat,

thinks of the congregation
gathered beyond town,
wind-whipped, looking for warm
words from his dazed lips.

No brand from the burning;
a thick man with a day's travel
caked on him like salt,

a preacher, one of those scattered like thistle
from the many-angled home chapel
facing all ways on its slabbed upland.

341

US 1st Division Airborne Ranger at rest in Honduras

The long arm hangs flat to his lap.
The relaxed wrist-joint is tender, shade-
cupped at the base of the thumb.

That long, drab line of American cloth,
those flat brows knitting a crux,
the close-shaven scalp, cheeks, jawbone and lips

rest in abeyance here, solid impermanence
like the stopped breath of a runner swathed up
in tinfoil bodybag, back from the front.

He rests, coloured like August foliage and earth
when the wheat's cropped, and the massive harvesters
go out on hire elsewhere,

his single-lens perspex eyeswield pushed up, denting
the folds of his skull stubble, his cap
shading his eyes which are already shaded
by bone. His pupils are shuttered,
the lenses widening inwards,
notions of a paling behind them.

One more for the beautiful table

Dense slabs of braided-up lupins –
someone's embroidery – Nan,
liking the blue,

one more for the beautiful table
with roses and handkerchiefs, seams
on the web of fifty five-year-olds' life-spans.

New, tough little stitches
run on the torn
wedding head-dresses.
No one can count them
back to the far-off
ghosts of the children's conceptions.

Those party days:

one more for the beautiful table

the extinction of breath in a sash.

What looks and surprises!
Nan on her bad legs
resumes the filminess of petals
and quotes blood pricks and blood stains

faded to mauve and to white and to crisp
brown drifts beneath bare sepals –

look, they have washed out.

Lambkin

(a poem in mother dialect)

That's better, he says, he says
that's better.

Dense slabs of braided-up lupins –
someone's embroidery – Nan,
liking the blue,

Oh you're a tinker, that's what you are,
a little tinker, a tinker, that's what you are.

One more for the beautiful table
with roses and handkerchiefs, seams
on the web of fifty five-year-olds' life-spans.

Come on now, come on, come on now,
come on, come on, come on now,

new tough little stitches
run on the torn
wedding head-dresses.
The children count them
back to the far-off
ghosts of their own conceptions.

Oh you like that, I know, yes,
you kick those legs, you kick them,
you kick those fat legs then.

Those party days

one more for the beautiful table

set out in the hall.

You mustn't have any tears, you're my good boy
aren't you my little good boy.

What looks and surprises!
Nan on her bad legs
resumes the filminess of petals,

she'll leave it to Carlie
her bad spice.

Let's wipe those tears, let's wipe off all those tears.
That's better, he says, he says
that's right.

She quotes blood pricks and bloodstains
faded to mauve and to white and to crisp
brown drifts beneath bare sepals –

look, they have washed out.

The green recording light falters
as if picking up voices

it's pure noise grain and nothing more human.
It's all right lambkin I've got you I've got you.

Dublin 1971

The grass looks different in another country.
By a shade more or a shade less, it startles
as love does in the sharply-tinged landscape
of sixteen to eighteen. When it is burnt
midsummer and lovers have learned to make love
with scarcely a word said, then they see nothing
but what is closest: an eyelash tonight,
the slow spread of a sweat stain,
the shoe-sole of the other as he walks off
watched from the mattress.

The top deck of the bus babbles with diplomats'
children returning from school, their language
an overcast August sky which can't clear.
Each syllable melting to static
troubles the ears of strangers, no stranger
but less sure than the stick-limbed children.
With one silvery, tarnishing ring between them
they walk barefoot past the Martello tower
at Sandymount, and wish the sea clearer,
the sun for once dazzling, fledged
from its wet summer nest of cloud-strips.

They make cakes of apple peel and arrowroot
and hear the shrieks of bold, bad seven-year-old Seamus
who holds the pavement till gone midnight
for all his mother's forlorn calling.
The freedom of no one related for thousands of miles,
the ferry forever going backward and forward
from rain runnel to drain cover...

The grass looks different in another country,
sudden and fresh, waving, unfurling
the last morning they see it, as they go down
to grey Dún Laoghaire by taxi.
They watch the slate rain coming in eastward
pleating the sea not swum in,
blotting the Ballsbridge house with its soft sheets
put out in the air to sweeten.

The hard-hearted husband

'Has she gone then?' they asked,
stepping round the back of the house
whose cat skulked in the grass.

She'd left pegs dropped in the bean-row,
and a mauve terrycloth babygrow
stirred on the line as I passed.

Her damsons were ripe and her sage was in flower,
her roses tilted from last night's downpour,
her sweetpeas and sunflowers leaned anywhere.

'She got sick of it, then,' they guessed,
and wondered if the torn-up paper
might be worth reading, might be a letter.

'It was the bills got her,' they knew,
seeing brown envelopes sheared with the white
in a jar on the curtainless windowsill,

some of them sealed still, as if she was through
with trying to pay, and would sit, chilled,
ruffling and arranging them like flowers
in the long dusks while the kids slept upstairs.

The plaster was thick with her shadows,
damp and ready to show
how she lived there and lay fallow

and how she stood at her window
and watched tall pylons stride down the slope
sizzling faintly, stepping away
as she now suddenly goes,

too stubborn to be ghosted at thirty.
She will not haunt here. She picks up her dirty
warm children and takes them

down to the gate which she lifts as it whines
and sets going a thin cry in her.
He was hard-hearted and no good to her
they say now, grasping the chance to be kind.

Malta

The sea's a featureless blaze.
On photographs nothing comes out
but glare, with that scarlet-rimmed fishing boat
far-off, lost to the lens.

At noon a stiff-legged tourist in shorts
steps, camera poised. He's stilted
as a flamingo, pink-limbed.

Icons of Malta gather around him.
He sweats as a procession passes
and women with church-dark faces
brush him as if he were air.

He holds a white crocheted dress
to give to his twelve-year-old daughter
who moons in the apartment, sun-sore.
The sky's tight as a drum, hard
to breathe in, hard to walk under.

He would not buy 'bikini for daughter'
though the man pressed him, with plump fingers
spreading out scraps of blue cotton.

Let her stay young, let her know nothing.
Let her body remain skimpy and sudden.
His wife builds arches of silence over her
new breasts and packets of tampons marked 'slender'.

At nights, when they think she's asleep,
they ache in the same places
but never louder than a whisper.

He watches more women melt into a porch.
Their white, still laundry flags from window to window
while they are absent, their balconies blank.

At six o'clock, when he comes home and snicks
his key in the lock so softly neither will catch it
he hears one of them laugh.
They are secret in the kitchen, talking of nothing,
strangers whom anyone might love.

Candlemas

Snowdrops, Mary's tapers,
barely alight in the grey shadows,

Candlemas in a wet February,
the soil clodded and frostless,
the quick blue shadows of snowlight again missed.

The church candles' mass
yellow as mothering bee cells,
melts to soft puddles of wax,

the snowdrops, with crisp ruffs
and green spikes clearing the leaf debris

are an unseen nebula
caught by a swinging telescope,

white tapers
blooming in structureless dusk.

Pilgrims

Let us think that we are pilgrims
in furs on this bleak water.
The *Titanic*'s lamps hang on its sides like fruit
on lit cliffs. We're shriven for rescue.

The sea snaps at our caulking.
We bend to our oars and praise God
and flex our fingers to bring
a drowned child out from the tarpaulin.

We're neither mothers nor fathers, but children,
fearful and full of trust,
lamblike as the *Titanic* goes down
entombing its witnesses.

We row on in a state of grace
in our half-empty lifeboats, sailing
westward for America, pilgrims,
numb to the summer-like choir
of fifteen hundred companions.

An Irish miner in Staffordshire

On smooth buttercup fields
the potholers sink down like dreams
close to Roman lead-mining country.

I sink the leafless shaft of an hydrangea twig
down through the slippy spaces I've made for it.
Dusted with hormone powder, moist,
its fibrous stem splays into root.

I graze the soft touches of compost
and wash them off easily, balled
under the thumb – clean dirt.
There's the man who gave me my Irish name

still going down, wifeless, that miner
who shafted the narrow cuffs of the earth
as if it was this he came for.

The Sea Skater

(1986)

For Francis, Ollie and Patrick

The bride's nights in a strange village

At three in the morning
while mist limps between houses
while cloaks and blankets
dampen with dew

the bride sleeps with her husband
bundled in a red blanket,
her mouth parts and a bubble
of sour breathing goes free.
She humps wool up to her ears
while her husband tightens his arms
and rocks her, mumbling. Neither awakes.

In the second month of the marriage
the bride wakes after midnight.
Damp-bodied
she lunges from sleep
hair pricking with sweat
breath knocking her sides.
She eels from her husband's grip
and crouches, listening.

The night is enlarged by sounds.
The rain has started.
It threshes leaves secretively
and there in the blackness
of whining dogs it finds out the house.
Its hiss enfolds her, blots up
her skin, then sifts off, whispering
in her like mirrors
the length of the rainy village.

Lazarus

Dumb, his lips swathed,
lips peaceful and dry

out of the swash and backwash of speech,

his face bound with a napkin,
his arms and his legs with gravecloths
in glistening daylight,

in dumbness, silky as flints
packed into chalk cliffs.

The age of the iron man
finished, the age of the stone
still blooming. Here are the avenues,
peaceful avenues with stone petals.

Here is a red-veined marble, and there
the white Carrara with black tracing

and all the messages, the pollen
on which passersby hang, bee-like,

words joined onto words.

Dumb, his lips sealed
with mouth-to-mouth breathing,

he abhors earth music:
the midday, dwindling
shadow of requiems.

A life-size statue of limestone,
scaly and worn over nostril
and lip-arches,

with yellow lichen and snails
poured into his eyes.

Liquid oboe pulsations
trail him, but dumbly
he pedals his stone body onward

past stab after word-covered slab
towards the expressionless sea he loves best,

to Bethsaida from Bethany.

Christmas roses

I remember years ago, that we had Christmas roses:
cold, greeny things under the snow –
fantastic hellebores, harbingers
of the century's worst winter.

On little fields stitched over with drystone
we broke snow curds, our sledge
tossing us out at the wall.

For twelve years a plateau of sea
stopped at my parents' window.
Here the slow Flatholm foghorn
sucking at the house fabric

recalls my little month-old brother,
kept in the house for weeks
while those snow days piled up like plates
to an impossible tower.

They were building the match factory
to serve moors seeded with conifers
that year of the Bay of Pigs,

the year of Cuba, when adults muttered
of taking to the moors with a shotgun
when the bomb dropped.

Such conversation, rapaciously
stored in a nine-year-old's memory
breeds when I stare down Bridgwater Bay
to that glassy CEGB elegance, Hinkley
Point, treating the landscape like snow,
melting down marshes and long, lost
muddy horizons.

Fir thickets replace those cushions
of scratchy heather, and prick out the noise
of larks in the air, so constant
I never knew what it was.

Little hellebores with green veins,
not at all tender, and scentless
on frosty ground, with your own small
melt, your engine of growth:
that was the way I liked you.

I imagine you sent back from Africa

I imagine you sent back from Africa
leaving a patchwork of rust and khaki
sand silt in your tea and your blood.

The metal of tanks and cans
puckers your taste-buds.
Your tongue jumps from the touch
of charge left in a dying battery.

You spread your cards in the shade
of roving lorries whose canvas
tents twenty soldiers.
The greased cards patter
in chosen spaces.

I imagine you sent back from Africa
with a tin mug kept for the bullet hole
in at one angle and out another.

You mount the train at the port
asking if anywhere on earth
offers such grey, mild people.

Someone draws down the blind.
You see his buttons, his wrist,
his teeth filled to the roots.
He weakens the sunlight for you
and keeps watch on your face.
Your day sinks in a hollow of sleep
racket and megaphoned voices.

The troop-ship booms once. Laden
with new men she moves down the Sound
low in the water, egg-carrying.

But for you daylight
with your relieved breath
supping up train dirt.
A jolt is a rescue from sleep
and a glaze of filth from the arm-rest
patches your cheek. You try to catch voices
calling out stations closer to home.

The knight

In the dusk of a forest chapel
a knight lies bleeding.

The edges of his wound are rawly
exhausted by blood chafing
but still the blood gathers and wells.

At first he lay with his arms folded
waiting for his brother officers
his dog curled at his feet,

but soon the dog with a whimper
made off, tearing its fur,
and soon the knight, moaning,
tried to cuddle into a foetal position
but the terrible wound prevented him.

His armour has become a bandage
as stiff as the casing of a chrysalis.
His face no longer has the strength for amazement.

The knight cries for his mother
in the dark of a forest chapel.
He wants the smell of her
and of all living things
which are not bleeding.

The scent and hissing of pine needles
make him believe he's in a hospital
where nurses pass by him.
He is afraid of falling
and of the stone floor under him.

In the dusk of a forest chapel
a knight lies bleeding.
In search of comfort
he turns to the warmer

grain of the wooden
bench he lies on
and licks its salty
whorls with his tongue.

In memoriam Cyril Smith 1913-1945

I've approached him since childhood,
since he was old, blurred,

my stake in the playground chants
and war games,

a word like 'brother'
mixed with a death story.

Wearing shorts and a smile
he stayed in the photograph box.

His hair was receding early.
He had Grandpa's long lip and my mother's love.

The jungle obliterates a city
of cries and murmurs,
bloody discharges
and unsent telegrams.

Now he is immanent

breaking off thoughts

printing that roll of film
one sweaty evening,

Four decades
have raised a thicket of deaths around him

a fence of thorn and a fence of roses.

His mother, my grandmother,
his father, his brother,

his camp companions

his one postcard.

The circle closes
in skin, limbs
and new resemblances.

We wanted to bring him
through life with us

but he grows younger.

We've passed him
holding out arms.

The parachute packers

The parachute packers with white faces
swathed over with sleep
and the stale bodily smell of sheets

make haste to tin huts where a twelve-hour
shift starts in ten minutes.
Their bare legs pump bicycle pedals,
they clatter on wooden-soled sandals
into the dazzling light over the work benches.

They rub in today's issue of hand-cream.
Their fingers skim on the silk
as the unwieldy billows of parachute flatten
like sea-waves, oiled, folded in sevens.

The only silk to be had
comes in a military packaging:
dull-green, printed, discreet,
gone into fashioning parachutes
to be wondered at like the flowers'
down-spinning, seed-bearing canopies
lodged in the silt of village memory.

A girl pulling swedes in a field
senses the shadow of parachutes
and gapes up, knees braced
and hair tangling. She must be riddled,
her warm juices all spilled
for looking upwards too early
into the dawn, leafy with parachutes.

Heavenly wide canopies
bring down stolid chaps with their rifle butts
ready to crack, with papers
to govern the upturned land,
with boots, barbed wire and lists on fine paper
thousands of names long.

I look up now at two seagulls,
at cloud drifts and a lamp-post
bent like a feeding swan,

and at the sound of needles
seaming up parachutes in Nissen huts
with a hiss and pull through the stuff
of these celestial ball-dresses

for nuns, agents, snow-on-the-boots men
sewn into a flower's corolla
to the music of *Workers' Playtime.*

At dusk the parachute packers
release their hair from its nets
and ride down lanes whitened by cow-parsley
to village halls, where the dances
and beer and the first cigarettes
expunge the clouds of parachute silk
and rules touching their hair and flesh.

In the bar they're the girls who pack parachutes
for our boys. They can forget
the coughs of the guard on duty,
the boredom and long hours
and half-heard cries of caught parachutists.

Porpoise washed up on the beach

After midday the great lazy
slaps of the sea,
the whistling of a boy who likes the empty
hour while the beach is feeding,

the cliffs vacant, gulls untidily drowsing
far out on the water.

I walked on in the dazzle
round to the next cove
where the sea was running backwards like mercury
from people busy at cutting
windows in the side of a beached porpoise.

The creature had died recently.
Naturally its blood was mammalian,
its skin supple and tough; it made me
instantly think of uses for it –
shoe soling, sealing the hulls of boats –
something to explain the intent knives
and people swiftly looking at me.

But there was no mussel harvest on the rocks
or boat blinding through noon
out to the crab pots,
not here but elsewhere the settled
stupor of digestion went on.

The porpoise had brought the boys between fourteen and eighteen,
lengthened their lives by a burning
profitless noon-time,
so they cut windows out of surprise
or idleness, finding the thing here
like a blank wall, inviting them.

They jumped from its body, prodded it,
looked in its mouth and its eyes,
hauled up its tail like a child's drawing
and became serious.

Each had the use of the knife in turn
and paused over the usual graffiti
to test words first with a knife-point
and fit the grey boulder of flesh under them.

Clapping their wings the gulls came back from the sea,
the pink screens of the hotel opened,
the last boy scoured the knife with sand.

I walked back along the shingle
breathing away the bloody trail of the porpoise
and saw the boys' wet heads glittering,
their hooting, diving
bodies sweeping them out of the bay.

In deep water

For three years I've been wary of deep water.
I busied myself on the shore
towelling, handing out underwear
wading the baby knee-high.

I didn't think I had forgotten
how to play in the deep water,
but it was only today I went there
passing the paddle boats and bathers,
the parallel harbour wall,
until there was no one at all but me
rolling through the cold water
and scarcely bothering to swim
from pure buoyancy.

Of course I could still see them:
the red and the orange armbands,
the man smiling and pointing seawards,
the tender faces.

It's these faces that have taken me
out of the deep water
and made my face clench like my mother's
once, as I pranced on a ten-foot
wall over a glass-house.

The water remembers my body,
stretched and paler as it is.
Down there is my old reflection
spread-eagled, steadily moving.

Lady Macduff and the primroses

Now the snowdrop, the wood-anemone, the crocus
have flowered
and faded back to dry, scarcely-seen threads,

Lady Macduff goes down to the meadow
where primrose flowers are thickening.

Her maid told her this morning, It's time
to pick them now, there will never be more
without some dying.

Even the kitchen girls, spared for an hour,
come to pick flowers for wine.

The children's nurse has never seemed to grasp
that she only need lay down the flowers loosely,

the flat-bottomed baskets soon fill
with yellow, chill primroses covered by sturdy leaves,

but the nurse will weave posies
even though the children are impatient
and only care who is first, has most
of their mother's quick smile.

Pasties have been brought from the castle.
Savoury juices spill from their ornate crusts,
white cloths are smeared with venison gravy
and all eat hungrily
out in the spring wind.

Lady Macduff looks round at the sparkling
sharpness of grass, whipped kerchiefs and castle battlements
edged with green light

and the primroses like a fall
colder than rain, warmer than snow,
petals quite still, hairy stems helplessly curling.

She thinks how they will be drunk
as yellow wine, swallow by swallow
filling the pauses of mid-winter,
sweet to raw throats.

Mary Shelley

In the weightlessness of time and our passage within it
voices and rooms swim.
Cleft after soft cleft
parts, word-covered lips
thin as they speak.

I should recall how pink and tender
your lids looked when you read too long
while I produced seamed
patchwork, my own phantom.

Am I the jury, the evidence,
the recollection?

Last night I dreamed of a prospect
and so I dreamed backwards:

first I woke in the dark
scraping my knuckles on board and mould.

I remember half listening
or reading in the shadow of a fire;
each evening I would lie quietly
breathing the scent of my flesh till I slept.

I loved myself in my new dress.
I loved the coral stems rising from the rosebush
under my window in March.
I was intact, neat,
dressing myself each morning.

I dreamed my little baby was alive,
mewing for me from somewhere in the room.
I chafed her feet and tucked her nightdress close.

Claire, Shelley and I left England.
We crossed the Channel and boasted afterwards
of soaked clothes, vomit and cloudbursts.

We went by grey houses, shutters still closed,
people warmly asleep. My eyes were dazed
wide open in abatement and vacancy.

*

A bad wife is like winter in the house.
(diary of Claire Clairmont, Florence 1820)

In Florence in winter grit scoured between houses;
the plaster needed replacing, the children had coughs.

I lived in a nursery which smelled of boredom and liniment.
In bed I used to dream of water crossings
by night. I looked fixedly forward.
It was the first winter I became ugly:
I was unloving all winter,
frozen by my own omens.

In Lerici I watched small boats on the bay
trace their insect trails on the flat water.
Orange lamps and orange blossom
lit and suffused the night garden.

Canvas slashed in a squall.
Stifling tangles of sail and fragile
masts snapping brought the boat over.
The blackened sea
kept its waves still, then tilting
knocked you into its cold crevices.

I was pressed to a pinpoint,
my breath flat.
Scarcely pulsating
I gave out nothing.

I gave out nothing before your death.
We would pass in the house with blind-lipped
anger in me.
You put me aside for the winter.

I would soften like a season
I would moisten and turn to you.
I would not conform my arms to the shapes of dead children.

I patched my babies and fed them
but death got at them.
Your eyes fed everywhere.

I wonder at bodies once clustered,
at delicate tissue
emerging unable to ripen.

Each time I returned to life
calmer than the blood which left me
weightless as the ticking of a blind-cord.
Inside my amply-filled dress
I am renewed seamlessly.

Fledged in my widow's weeds
I was made over, for this
prickle of live flesh
wedged in its own corpulence.

The plum tree

The plum was my parents' tree,
above them
as I was at my bedroom window
wondering why they chose to walk this way quietly
under the plum tree.

My sisters and I stopped playing
as they reached up and felt for the fruit.
It lay among bunches of leaves,
oval and oozing resin
out into pearls of gum.
They bit into the plums
without once glancing
back at the house.

Some years were thin:
white mildew streaking the trunk,
fruit buckled and green,

but one April
the tree broke from its temperate blossoming
and by late summer the branches
trailed earth, heavy with pound
after pound of bursting Victorias,

and I remember the oblivious steps
my parents took as they went quietly
out of the house one summer evening
to stand under the plum tree.

The air-blue gown

Tonight I'm eating the past
consuming its traces,

the past is a heap
sparkling with razor blades
where patches of sweetness
deepen to compost,

woodlice fold up their legs
and roll luxuriously,

cold vegetation
rises to blood heat.

The local sea's bare
running up to the house

tufting its waves
with red seaweed
spread against a Hebridean noon.

Lightly as sandpipers marking the shoreline
boats at the jetty sprang
and rocked upon the green water.

Not much time passes, but suddenly
now when you're crumpled after a cold
I see how the scale and changes
of few words measure us.

At this time of year I remember a cuckoo's
erratic notes on a mild morning.
It lay full-fed on a cherry branch
repeating an hour of sweetness
its grey body unstirring
its lustrous eyes turning.

Talk sticks and patches
walls and the kitchen formica
while at the table outlines
seated on a thousand evenings
drain like light going out of a landscape.

The back door closes, swings shut,
drives me to place myself inside it.
In this flickering encampment
fire pours sideways
then once more stands
evenly burning.

I wake with a touch on my face
and turn sideways
butting my head into darkness.

The wind's banging diminishes. An aircraft
wanders through the upper atmosphere
bee-like, propelled by loneliness.
It searches for a fallen corolla,
its note rising and going
as it crosses the four quarters.

The city turns a seamed cheek upward,
confides itself to the sound and hazardous
construction of a journey by starlight.

I drop back soundlessly,
my lips slackened.
Headache alone is my navigator,
plummeting, shedding its petals.

It's Christmas Eve.
Against my nightdress a child's foot, burning,
passes its fever through the cotton,

the tide of bells swings
and the child winces.

The bells are shamelessly
clanging, the voices
hollering churchward.

I'm eating the past tonight
tasting gardenia perfume
licking the child-like socket of an acorn
before each is consumed.

It was not Hardy who stayed there
searching for the air-blue gown.
It was the woman who once more, secretly,
tried the dress on.

My sad descendants

O wintry ones, my sad descendants,
with snowdrops in your hands you join me
to celebrate these dark, short
days lacking a thread of sun.

Three is a virtuous number,
each time one fewer to love,
the number of fairy tales,
wishes, labours for love.

My sad descendants
who had no place in the sun,
hope brought you to mid-winter,
never to spring
or to the lazy benches of summer
and old bones.

My sad descendants
whose bones are a network of frost,
I carry your burn and your pallor,
your substance dwindled to drops.

I breathe you another pattern
since no breath warmed you from mine,
on the cold of the night window
I breathe you another pattern,

I make you outlive rosiness
and envied heartbeats.

Patrick at four years old on Bonfire Night

Cursing softly and letting the matches drop
too close to the firework box,
we light an oblation
to rough-scented autumnal gods,
shaggy as chrysanthemums;

and you, in your pearly maroon
waterproof suit, with your round
baby brows, stare upward and name
chrysanthemum fountain and silver fountain
and Catherine wheel: saints' names
like yours, Patrick, and you record them.
This morning, climbing up on my pillow,
you list saints' names guessed at from school.

They go off, one by one on the ritual plank:
jack-in-a-box, high-jump and Roman candle,
searching the currant bushes with gunpowder.

We stand in savoury fumes like pillars,
our coats dark, our slow-burning fuse lit,
and make our little bonfire with spits
for foil-wrapped potatoes and hot-dogs –

by your bedtime
the rough-scented autumnal gods
fuse with the saints and jack-lanterns.

The horse landscape

Today in a horse landscape
horses steam in the lee of thorn hedges
on soaking fields. Horses waltz
on iron poles in dank fairgrounds.

A girl in jodhpurs on Sand Bay
leads her pony over and over
jumps made of driftwood and traffic cones,

A TV blares the gabble of photofinishes.
The bookie's plastic curtain releases
punters onto the hot street
littered with King Cone papers.

In a landscape with clouds and chalk downs
and cream houses, a horse rigid as bone
glares up at kites and hang-gliders.

One eye's cut from the flowered turf:
a horse skull, whispering secrets
with wind-sighs like tapping on phone wires.

The group leader in beautiful boots
always on horse-back,
the mounted lady squinnying
down at the hunt intruders,
draw blood for their own horse landscape
and scorn horse-trading, letting the beasts mate
on scrubby fields, amongst catkins
and watery ditches.

Here's a rearing bronze horse
welded to man, letting his hands
stay free for banner and weapon –
mild shadow of Pushkin's nightmare.

Trained police horses sway on great hooves.
Riders avoid our faces, and gaze
down on our skull crowns
where the bone jigsaw cleaves.

Grooms whistle and urge
the sweaty beasts to endure battle.
We're always the poor infantry
backing off Mars field,
out of frame for the heroic riders
preserved in their horse landscape.

Thetis

Thetis, mother of all mothers
who fear the death of their children,
held down her baby Achilles
in the dark Styx

whose waters flow fast
without ripples or wave-break,
bearing little boats of paper
with matchstick masts,
returning not even a sigh
or drenched fibre to life.

Thetis, mother of all mothers
destined to outlive their children,
took Achilles by the heel
and thrust him into the Styx

so that sealed, immortal, dark-eyed,
he'd return to his white cradle
and to his willow rattle.

She might have held him less tightly
and for a while given him
wholly to the trustworthy river
which has no eddies or backwaters
and always carries its burdens onward,
she might have left him to play
on the soft grass of the river-edge.

But through the pressure-marks of her white fingers
the baby found his way forward
towards the wound he knew best.
Even while the arrow was in the wood
and the bow gleaming with leaves
the current of the Styx
faintly suckled and started
in the little flexed ankles
pressed against Thetis' damp breasts.

In the tents

Our day off, agreed by the wind
and miry fields and unburied dead,
in the tent with first light filtering
a rosy dawn which masks rain.

The rosiness rests on our damp flesh,
on armour stacked by the tent walls,
on our captain and his lolling companion.

I go down to the sea shore
to find white pebbles for games.
I look for the island, kidding myself
I see it hump through the waves.

Back in the tent it's warm, wine-smelling,
heavy with breath.
The lamp shines on the bodies
of our captain and his companion.

These are the tented days I remember
more than the battles.
This is the smell of a herbal rub
on great Achilles.
This is the blue soap-scum on the pitcher,
and cold parcels of goat-meat,
the yawning moment
late in the evening, when I step out
and see the stars alight in their same places.

Uncle Will's telegram

She kept Uncle Will's telegram
between the sheets of her wedding-album.
Her life-long imaginary future
dazzled the moment it came.

He tried the counter-top biro
and asked the post office clerk
to check the time of arrival
for ten words in block capitals.

In the levelled-down churchyard
they posed for the first photographs
while powdery grandmothers
whispered 'We wish you'
and came up with the word 'Happiness'.

She stood against laurel-black cherries
while the church dived into silence,
a great maritime creature

leaving without echoes.
At the lych-gate a tide-line
of white flowers remained.

In the Flowers the best man
read Uncle Will's telegram
and the guests lifted their glasses
shouting 'Io, Io Hymen!'

Rapunzel

Rapunzel
let down your hair,

let your strong hair
wind up the water you wish for.

All your life looking down
on bright tree-tops
your days go by quickly.

You read and you eat
in your white tower top
where sunlight fans through high
windows and far below you
bushes are matted with night.

With soft thumbprints
darkness muddles your pages.
The prince arrives,
whose noisy breathing
and sweat as he vaults your window-sill
draw you like wheat fields
on the enchanted horizontal.

He seeds your body with human fragments,
dandruff, nail-clippings, dust.
The detritus of new pleasures
falls on your waxed boards.

Your witch mother, sweeping them,
sorrowfully banishes the girl
who has let a prince clamber her.

For six years you wander the desert
from level to pale level.
At night you make a bunker to sleep in
near to the coyotes.

The ragged prince plays blind-man's-buff
to the sound of your voice singing
as you gather desert grasses
in hollows hidden from him.

Daily your wise mother
unpicks the walls of the tower.
Its stones are taken for sheep-folds,
your circle of hair
hidden beneath the brambles.

Bewick's swans

Ahead of us, moving through time
with a skein's precision and mystery
over the navy spaces of winter
the inter-continental migration continues.

It starts on one moment
of one season, when time ripens
down to the soft dawn chill on a feather

or the germ sprouting in winter wheat
ready to be grazed by the wild swans.

Hour by hour the birds move up the wedge
until they fly at its point, in the keen
apex, the buffet of wind.
A dark triangle of birds streams backward
and peels away and reforms like rain on glass.

Sometimes they fall almost to the white waves
then stretch their necks and call and begin
the long pull onward, leaving a swan plunged
like an untidy bundle of sheets
swept in a ship's backwash.

See them nose the long coastline
in a glide of perfected instinct.
To their preferred feeding-grounds
they are a long arrow
shot from unimaginable nowhere.
Here they are keeled, treading
the known roughness of grass tussocks.

The private swans arch out their feathers
and preen and nourish themselves.
The mild floodlights each night
and people gathered to watch
are no stranger to the swans than the prickle
of green waiting in the wheat stripes each winter.

The sea skater

A skater comes to this blue pond,
his worn Canadian skates
held by the straps.

He sits on the grass
lacing stiff boots
into a wreath of effort and breath.

He tugs at the straps and they sound
as ice does when weight troubles it
and cracks bloom around stones

creaking in quiet mid-winter
mid-afternoons: a fine time for a skater.
He knows it and gauges the sun
to see how long it will be safe to skate.

Now he hisses and spins in jumps
while powder ice clings to the air
but by trade he's a long-haul skater.

Little villages, stick-like in the cold,
offer a child or a farm-worker
going his round. These watch him
go beating onward between iced alders
seawards, and so they picture him
always smoothly facing forward, foodless and waterless,
mounting the crusted waves on his skates.

In the tea house

In the tea house the usual
customers sit with their cooling
tea glasses
and new pastries
sealed at the edge
with sticky droplets.

The waitress walks off,
calves solid and shapely as vases,
leaving a juicy baba
before her favourite.

Each table has bronze or white chrysanthemums
and the copper glass-stands imperceptibly
brush each other like crickets
suddenly focussed at dusk,

but the daily newspapers
dampened by steam
don't rustle.

The tea house still has its blinds out
even though the sun is now amiably
yellow as butter

and people hurrying by raise up their faces
without abandon, briskly
talking to their companions;

no one sits out at the tables
except a travel-stained couple
thumbing a map.

The waitress reckons her cloths
watching the proprietor
while he, dark-suited, buoyant,
pauses before a customer.

Her gaze breaks upon the tea-house
like incoming water
joining sandbanks swiftly and
softly moving the pebbles,

moving the coloured sugar and coffee
to better places,
counting the pastries.

Florence in permafrost

Cold pinches the hills around Florence.
It roots out vines, truffles for lemon trees
painfully heated by charcoal
to three degrees above freezing.

A bristling fir forest
moves forward over Tuscany.
A secret wood
riddled with worm and lifeless
dust-covered branches
stings the grass and makes it flowerless,

freezing the long-closed eyelids of Romans.
They sleep entrusted to darkness
in the perpetual, placid, waveless
music of darkness.

The forest ramps over frontiers and plains
and swallows voluble Customs men
in slow ash. A wind sound
scrapes its thatching of sticks.

Blind thrushes in the wood blunder
and drop onto the brown needles.
There are no nests or singing-places.

A forest of matchwood and cheap furniture
marches in rows. Nobody harvests
its spongey woods and makes the trunks sigh
like toy soldiers giving up life.

All over Italy and northward
from fair Florence to München
and the cold city of Potsdam
the forest spreads like a pelt
on meadows, terraces, riverbanks
and the shards of brick houses.

It hides everywhere from everywhere
as each point of perspective
is gained by herds of resinous firs.

There may be human creatures
at nest in the root sockets.
They whicker words to each other
against the soughing of evergreens
while the great faces of reindeer
come grazing beside the Arno.

Missile launcher passing at night

The soft fields part in hedges, each
binds each, copse pleats
rib up the hillside.

Darkness is coming and grass
bends downward.
The cattle out all night
eat, knee-deep, invisible
unless a headlight arcs on their mild faces.

The night's damp fastens, droplet by droplet,
onto the animals.
They vibrate to the passing of a missile launcher
and stir
their patient eyelashes.

A blackbird
startled by floodlights
reproduces morning.

Cattle grids tremble and clang,
boots scrape
holly bursts against wet walls
lost at the moment of happening.

The Apple Fall

(1983)

For my parents

The marshalling yard

In the goods yard the tracks are unmarked.
Snow lies, the sky is full of it.
Its hush swells in the dark.

Grasped by black ice on black
a massive noise of breathing
fills the tracks;

cold women, ready for departure
smooth their worn skirts
and ice steals through their hands like children
from whose touch they have already been parted.

Now like a summer
the train comes
beating the platform
with its blue wings.

The women stir. They sigh.
Feet slide
warm on a wooden stairway
then a voice calls and
milk drenched with aniseed
drawls on the walk to school.

At last they leave.
Their breathless neighbours
steal from the woods, the barns,
and tender straw
sticks to their palms.

A cow here in the June meadow

A cow here in the June meadow
where clouds pile, tower above tower.

We lie, buried in sunburn,
our picnic a warm
paper of street tastes,

she like a gold cloud
steps, moony.
Her silky rump dips
into the grasses, buffeting
a mass of seed ready to run off in flower.

We stroll under the elder, smell
wine, trace blackfly along its leaf-veins

then burning and yawning we pile
kisses onto the hot upholstery.

Now evening shivers along the water surface.
The cow, suddenly planted stands – her tender
skin pollened all over –
ready to nudge all night at the cold grasses,
her udder heavily and more heavily swinging.

Zelda

At Great Neck one Easter
were Scott
Ring Lardner
and Zelda, who sat
neck high in catalogues like reading cards

her hair in curl for
wild stories, applauded.
A drink, two drinks and a kiss.

Scott and Ring both love her –
gold-headed, sky-high Miss
Alabama. (The lioness
with still eyes and no affectations
doesn't come into this.)

Some visitors said she ought
to do more housework, get herself taught
to cook.
Above all, find some silent occupation
rather than mess up Scott's vocation.

In France her barriers were simplified.
Her husband developed a work ethic:
film actresses; puritan elegance;

tipped eyes spilling material
like fresh Americas. You see
said Scott   they know about work, like me.

You can't beat a writer for justifying adultery.

Zelda
always wanted to be a dancer

she said, writhing
among the gentians that smelled of medicine.

A dancer in a sweat lather is not beautiful.
A dancer's mind can get fixed.

Give me a wooden floor, a practice dress,
a sheet of mirrors and hours of labour
and lie me with my spine to the floor
supple   secure.

She handed these back too
with her gold head and her senses.

She asks for visits. She makes herself hollow
with tears, dropped in the same cup.
Here at the edge of her sensations
there is no chance.

Evening falls on her Montgomery verandah.
No cars come by. Her only visitor
his voice, slender along the telephone wire.

Annunciation off East Street

The window swings and squeaks in the sun.
Mary says to the angel: 'Come.
My husband is sleepy.
You're rapid and warm-winged.'

First Elizabeth, breathless,
ties up her dates in her heart.
How can a woman be so fortunate?
'Precious baby,' they write on her chart.

Elizabeth the ageing primipara
reminded of her ancestress Sarah
who also slept with an old man.
Bearded, whuffling,
his flesh drew like chicken-skin.

Mary sat with Elizabeth
chopping up parsley, their breath
pregnant, settling the room.
Here Elizabeth crouched for six months
uterus bubbling
while Zacharias snipped the altar flame.

'So it turns out at last.
You and the holy spirit –
I guessed it.
We're both gigantic
at night, feeding our great babies.

I gorge where no one can see me,
count days, walk tiptoe
still fearing the bloody trickle.'

Mary answered her laughing:
'Elizabeth, let's tell them everything!'

The Polish husband

The traffic halted
and for a moment
the broad green avenue
hung like a wave

while a woman crossing
stopped me and said

'Can you show me my wedding?
– In which church is it going to be held?'

The lorries hooted at her
as she stood there on the island
for her cloak fell back
and under it her legs were bare.
Her hair was dyed blonde
and her sad face deeply tanned.

I asked her 'What is the name of your husband?'
She wasn't sure, but she knew his first name was Joe,
she'd met him in Poland
and this was the time for the wedding.

There was a cathedral behind us
and a sign to the centre of the town.
'I am not an expert on weddings,'
I said, 'but take that honey-coloured building
which squats on its lawns like a cat –
at least there's music playing inside it.'

So she ran with her heels tapping
and the long, narrow folds of her cloak falling apart.
A veil on wire flew from her head,
her white figure ducked in the porch and blew out.

But Joe, the Polish man. In the rush of this town
I can't say whether she even found him
to go up the incense-heavy church beside him
under the bridal weight of her clothes,
or whether he was one of the lorry drivers
to whom her brown, hurrying legs were exposed.

The damson

Where have you gone
small child,
the damson bloom
on your eyes

the still heap
of your flesh
lightly composed
in a grey shawl,

your skull's pulse
stains you,
the veins slip deep.

Two lights burn
at the mouth of the cave
where the air's thin
and the tunnels boom
with your slippery blood.

Your unripe cheeks cling
to the leaves, to the wall,
your grasp unpeels
and your bruises murmur

while blueness clouds
on the down of your eyes,
your tears erode
and your smile files

through your lips like a soldier
who shoots at the sky
and you flash up in silver;

where are you now
little one,
peeled almond,
damson bloom?

In Rodmell Garden

It's past nine and breakfast is over.
With morning frost on my hands I cross
the white grass, and go nowhere.

It's icy: domestic. A grain
of coffee burns my tongue. Its heat
folds into the first cigarette.

The garden and air are still.
I am a stone and the world falls from me.

I feel untouchable – a new planet
where life knows it isn't safe to begin.
From silver flakes of ash I shape
a fin and watch it with anguish.

I hear apples rolling above me;
November twigs; a bare existence –

my sister is a marvellous
dolphin, flanking her young.
Her blood flushes her skin

but mine is trapped. Occasional moments
allow me to bathe in their dumb sweetness.

My loose pips ripen. My night subsides
rushing, like the long glide of an owl.

Raw peace. A pale, frost-lit morning.
The black treads of my husband on the lawn
as he goes from the house to the loft
                    laying out apples.

The apple fall

In a back garden I'm painting
the outside toilet in shell and antelope.
The big domestic bramley tree
hangs close to me, rosy and leafless.
Sometimes an apple thumps
into the bushes I've spattered with turpentine
while my brush moves with a suck
over the burnt-off door frame.

Towels from the massage parlour
are out on the line next door:
all those bodies sweating into them
each day – the fabric stiffening –
towels bodiless and sex over.

I load the brush with paint again
and I hear myself breathing.
Sun slips off the wall
so the yard is cool
and lumbered with shadows,

and then a cannonade of apples
punches the wall and my arms,
the ripe stripes on their cheeks fall open,
flesh spurts and the juices fizz and glisten.

Pictures of a Chinese nursery

Yesterday my stepson came home with school photographs.
The image is altered:
no longer one child
rimmed with a photographer's background
smiling much as he does at home

but three or four placed at a table together
working at egg-boxes, tissue-paper
and friendship enough to shiver their absorbed faces.
'That's Jessica. Sometimes, she gives all of us a kiss.'
Others are pointed out for pissing in school flowerbeds.

On his wall I have stuck a poster of a Chinese nursery.
There is a river, a tree,
a wooden bridge, and far into the distance
thick-packed orchards fruiting and flowering.

On the verandah the children fall into place
as radiant parents stride to the field,

the nursery curls on itself
the day without clocks unfolds
and after dinner their songs fly onto the mountain
as far as the plum orchards where workers stop to eat rice.

Pharaoh's daughter

The slowly moving river in summer
where bulrushes, mallow and water forget-me-not
slip to their still faces.

A child's body
joins their reflections,

his plastic boat
drifts into midstream
and though I lean down to
brown water that smells of peppermint
I can't get at it:
my willow branch flails and pushes the boat outwards.

He smiles quickly
and tells me it doesn't matter;
my feet grip in the mud
and mash blue flowers under them.

Then we go home
masking with summer days the misery
that has haunted a whole summer.

I think once of the Egyptian woman
who drew a baby from the bulrushes
hearing it mew in the damp
odrorous growth holding its cradle.

There's nothing here but the boat
caught by its string
and through this shimmering day I struggle
drawn down by the webbed
years, the child's life cradled within.

Domestic poem

So, how decisive a house is:
quilted, a net of blood and green
droops on repeated actions at nightfall.

A bath run through the wall
comforts the older boy sleeping
meshed in the odours of breath and Calpol

while in the maternity hospital
ancillaries rinse out the blood bottles;

the feel and the spore
of babies' sleep stays here.

Later, some flat-packed plastic
swells to a parachute of oxygen
holding the sick through their downspin,

now I am well enough, I
iron, and place the folded sheets in bags
from which I shall take them, identical,
after the birth of my child.

And now the house closes us,
                    close on us,
like fruit we rest in its warm branches

and though it's time for the child to come
nobody knows it, the night passes

while I sleepwalk the summer heat.

Months shunt me and I bring you
like an old engine hauling the blue
spaces that flash between track and train time.

Mist rises, smelling of petrol's
burnt offerings, new born,

oily and huge, the lorries drum
on Stokes' Croft,

out of the bathroom mirror the sky
is blue and pale as a Chinese mountain.

and I breathe in.

It's time to go now. I take nothing
but breath, thinned.
A blown-out dandelion globe
might choose my laundered body to grow in.

Patrick I

Patrick, I cannot write
such poems for you as a father might
coming upon your smile,

your mouth half sucking, half sleeping,
your tears shaken from your eyes like sparklers
break up the nightless weeks of your life:

lighthearted, I go to the kitchen
and cook breakfast, aching as you grow hungry.
Mornings are plain as the pages
of books in sedentary schooldays.

If I were eighty and lived next door
hanging my pale chemises on the porch
would I envy or pity my neighbour?

Polished and still as driftwood
she stands smoothing her dahlias;

liquid, leaking,
I cup the baby's head to my shoulder:

the child's a boy and will not share
one day these obstinate, exhausted mornings.

Patrick II

The other babies were more bitter than you
Patrick, with your rare, tentative cry,
your hours of steep, snuffing the medical air.

Give me time for your contours, your fierce drinking.
Like land that has been parched for half a summer
and smiles, sticky with feeding

I have examined and examined you
at midnight, at two days; I have accompanied you
to the blue world on another floor of the hospital
where half-formed babies open their legs like anemones
and nurses, specialised as astronauts,
operate around the apnoea pillows.

But here you bloomed. You survived,
sticky with nectar. X-rayed, clarified,
you came back, dirty and peaceful.

And now like sunflowers settling their petals
for the last strokes of light in September
your eyes turn to me at 3 A.M.

You meet my stiff, mucousy face
and snort, beating your hand on my breast
as one more feed flows through the darkness, timed
to nothing now but the pull of your mouth.

Weaning

Cool as sleep, the crates ring.
Birds stir and my milk stings me;
you slip my grasp. I never find you
in dreams – only your mouth
not crying
your sleep still pressing on mine.

The carpets shush. The house back silences.
I turn with you, wide-lipped
blue figure

into the underground of babies
and damp mothers fumbling at bras

and the first callus grows on us
weaned from your night smiles.

Clinic day

The midwife whose omniscient hands
drew blood as I draw money out on Tuesdays
calls me to wait. We stand
half off the pavement, she spinning a bicycle pedal,
I rocking a pram.

She will be homeless she says by Friday.
But I can't help her. I want to respond to
her troubles with the sleeping flesh of the baby.
Useless. Her days of him are over.

Here at the clinic they know we are mothers.
I might avert all eyes from the baby,
tie a blue bead to his wrist,
not name him –

yet here they brazenly call him my son,
brandish his name on paper,
tell me how well he gets on.

Breathlessly evil fate stays
by their red door-posts on tiptoe:
they will not play.

Approaches to winter

Now I write off a winter of growth.
First, hands batting the air,
forehead still smeared,

– now, suddenly, he stands there
upright and rounded as a tulip.
The garden sparkles through the windows.

Dark and a heap in my arms;
the thermostat clicking all night.
Out in the road beached cars and winter
so cold five minutes would finish you.

Light fell in its pools
each evening. Tranquilly
it stamped the same circles.

Friends shifted their boots on the step.
Their faces gleamed from their scarves
that the withdrawal of day
brought safety.

Experience so stitched, intimate,
mutes me.
Now I'm desperate for solitude.
The house enrages me.

I go miles, pushing the pram,
thinking about Christina Rossetti's
black dresses – my own absent poems.

I go miles, touching his blankets proudly,
drawing the quilt to his lips.

I write of winter and the approaches to winter.
Air clings to me, rotten Lord Derbies,
patched in their skins, thud down.
The petals of Michaelmas daisies give light.

Now I'm that glimpsed figure for children
occupying doorways and windows;
that breath of succulence
ignored till nightfall.

I go out before the curtains are drawn
and walk close to the windows
which shine secretly.
Bare to the street
red pleats of a lampshade expose
bodies in classic postures, arguing.

Their senseless jokes explode with saliva.
I mop and tousle.

It's three o'clock in the cul-de-sac.
Out of the reach of traffic,
free from the ply
of bodies glancing and crossing,
the shopping, visiting,
cashing orders at the post office,

I lie on my bed in the sun
drawing down streams of babble.
This room holds me, a dull
round bulb stubbornly
rising year after year in the same place.

The night chemist

In the chemist's at night-time
swathed counters and lights turned down
lean and surround us.

Waiting for our prescriptions
we clock these sounds:
a baby's peaked hush,
hawked breath.

I pay a pound
and pills fall in my curled palms.
Holding their white packages tenderly
patients track back to the pain.

'Why is the man shouting?' Oliver asks me.
I answer, 'He wants to go home.'
Softly, muffled by cloth
the words still come
and the red-streaked drunkard goes past us,
rage scalding us.

I would not dare bring happiness
into the chemist's at night-time.
Its gift-wrapped lack of assistance still presses
as suffering closes the blinded windows.

St Paul's

This evening clouds darken the street quickly,
more and more grey
flows throngh the yellowing treetops,

traffic flies downhill
roaring and spangled with faces,
full buses
rock past the Sussex Place roundabout.

In Sussex the line of Downs
has no trees to uncover,
no lick of the town's wealth, blue
in smoke, no gold, fugitive dropping.
In villages old England
checks rainfall, sick of itself.

Here there are scraps and flashes:
bellying food smells – last-minute buying –
plantain, quarters of ham.
The bread shop lady pulls down
loaves that will make tomorrow's cheap line.

On offer are toothpaste and shoe soles
mended same day for Monday's interview
and a precise network of choices
for old women collecting their pension
on Thursday, already owing the rent man.

Some places are boarded. You lose your expectancy –
soon it appears you never get home. Still
it's fine on evenings and in October
to settle here. Still the lights splashing look beautiful.

Poem for December 28

My nephews with almond faces
black hair like bunces of grapes

    (the skin stroked and then bruised
    the head buried and caressed)

he takes his son's head in his hands
kisses it   blesses it   leaves it:

the boy with circles under his eyes like damsons
not the blond baby, the stepson.

In the forest stories about the black
father   the jew   the incubus

if there are more curses they fall on us.

Behind the swinging ropes of their isolation
my nephews wait, sucking their sweets.
The hall fills quickly and neatly.

If they keep still as water
    I'll know them.
I look but I can't be certain:

my nephews with heavy eyelids
blowing in the last touches of daylight

my sisters raising them up like torches.

Greenham Common

Today is barred with darkness of winter.
In cold tents women protest,
for once unveiled, eyes stinging with smoke.

They stamp round fires in quilted anoraks,
glamourless, they laugh often
and teach themselves to speak eloquently.
Mud and the camp's raw bones
set them before the television camera.

Absent, the women of old photographs
holding the last of their four children,
eyes darkened, hair covered,
bodies waxy as cyclamen;
absent, all these suffering ones.

New voices rip at the throat,
new costumes, metamorphoses.

Soft-skirted, evasive
women were drawn from the ruins,
swirls of ash on them like veils.

History came as a seducer
and said: this is the beauty of women
in bombfall. Dolorous
you curl your skirts over your sleeping children.

Instead they stay at this place
all winter; eat from packets and jars,
keep sensible, don't hunger,
battle each day at the wires.

Poem for hidden women

'Fuck this staring paper and table –
I've just about had enough of it.

I'm going out for some air,'
he says, letting the wind bang up his sheets of poems.

He walks quickly; it's cool,
and rainy sky covers both stars and moon.
Out of the windows come slight
echoes of conversations receding upstairs.

There. He slows down.
A dark side-street – thick bushes –
he doesn't see them.
He smokes. Leaves can stir as they please.

(We clack like jackrabbits from pool to pool of lamplight.
Stretching our lips, we walk exposed
as milk cattle past heaps of rubbish

killed by the edge
of knowledge that trees hide
a face slowly detaching itself
from shadow, and starting to smile.)

The poet goes into the steep alleys
close to the sea, where fish scales line the gutter
and women prostitute themselves to men
as men have described in many poems.

They've said how milky, or bitter
as lemons they find her –
the smell of her hair
...vanilla...cinnamon...
there's a smell for every complexion.

Cavafy tells us he went always
to secret rooms and purer vices;
he wished to dissociate himself
from the hasty unlacings of citizens
fumbling, capsizing –
white
flesh in a mound and kept from sight,

but he doesn't tell us
whether these boys' hair always smelled of cinnamon
or if their nights cost more than spices.

A woman goes into the night café,
chooses a clean
knife and a spoon
and takes up her tray.
Quickly the manageress leans from the counter.
(As when a policeman arrests a friend
her eyes plunge and her voice roughens.)
She points to a notice with her red nail:
'After 11 we serve only accompanied females.'

The woman fumbles her grip
on her bag, and it slips.
Her forces tumble.
People look on as she scrabbles
for money and tampax.
A thousand shadows accompany her
down the stiff lino, through the street lighting.

The poet sits in a harbour bar
where the tables are smooth and solid to lean on.
It's peaceful. Men gaze
for hours at beer and brass glistening.
The sea laps. The door swings.

The poet feels poems
invade him. All day he has been stone-breaking
he says. He would be happier in cafés
in other countries, drinking, watching;

he feels he's a familiar sort of poet
but he's at ease with it.
Besides, he's not actually writing a poem:
there's plenty, he's sure,
in drink and hearing the sea move.

For what is Emily Dickinson doing
back at the house – the home?
A doctor emerges, wiping his face,
and pins a notice on the porch.
After a while you don't even ask.

No history
gets at this picture:
a woman named Sappho
sat in bars by purple water
with her feet crossed at the ankles
and her hair flaming with violets
never smiling when she didn't feel like it.

'End here, it's hopeful,'
says the poet, getting up from the table.

If no revolution come

If no revolution come
star clusters
will brush heavy on the sky

and grapes burst
into the mouths of fifteen
well-fed men,

these honest men
will build them houses like pork palaces
if no revolution come,

short-life dust children
will be crumbling in the sun –
they have to score like this
if no revolution come.

The sadness of people
don't look at it too long:
you're studying for madness
if no revolution come.

If no revolution come
it will be born sleeping,
it will be heavy as baby
playing on mama's bones,

it will be gun-thumping on Sunday
and easy good time
for men who make money,

for men who make money
grow like a roof
so the rubbish of people
can't live underneath.

If no revolution come
star clusters
will drop heavy from the sky

and blood burst
out of the mouths of fifteen
washing women,

and the land-owners will drink us
one body by one:
they have to score like this
if no revolution come.

A safe light

I hung up the sheets in moonlight,
surprised that it really was so
steady, a quickly moving pencil

flowing onto the stained cotton.
How the valves
in that map
of taut fabric
blew in and blew out

then spread flat
over the tiles
while the moon filled them with light.

A hundred feet above the town
for once the moonscape showed nothing extraordinary

only the clicking pegs
and radio news from our kitchen.
One moth hesitated
tapping at our lighted window

and in the same way the moonlight
covered the streets, all night.

Near Dawlish

Her fast asleep face turns from me,
the oil on her eyelids gleams
and the shadow of a removed moustache
darkens the curve of her mouth,

her lips are still flattened together
and years occupy her face,
her holiday embroidery glistens,
her fingers quiver then rest.

I perch in my pink dress
sleepiness fanning my cheeks,
not lurching, not touching
as the train leaps.

Mother you should not be sleeping.
Look how dirty my face is, and lick
the smuts off me with your salt spit.

Golden corn rocks to the window
as the train jerks. Your narrowing body leaves me
frightened, too frightened to cry for you.

The last day of the exhausted month

The last day of the exhausted month
of August. Hydrangeas
purple and white like flesh immersed in water
with no shine
to keep the air off them
open their tepid petals more and more widely.

The newly-poured tar smells antiseptic
like sheets moulding on feverish skin:
surfaces of bedrock, glasslike passivity.

The last day of the exhausted month
goes quickly. A brown parcel
arrives with clothes left at the summer lodgings,
split and too small.
A dog noses
better not look at it too closely
God knows why they bothered to send them at all.

A smell of cat
joins us just before eating.

The cat is dead but its brown
smell still seeps from my tub of roses.

Second marriages

These second marriages arching within
smiles of their former friends:
his former wife and her child-swapping
remnants of weekday companionship,
her former husband, his regular
friends who encircled her
those wet Saturdays after the baby was born.

The children's early birthdays, the tea
and talk about socialisation;
the shared potties.
Frozen in these is the father's
morning exit from the maternity hospital.

Sliced from the album those gowns
that blood; the shawl in a heap,
those marital triumphant
glances at night when they got him to sleep.

Second marriages endure without these
public and early successes,
no longer tempting others or fate
by their caresses.

The deserted table

Coiled peel goes soft on the deserted table
where faïence, bubble glasses, and the rest
of riches thicken.

People have left their bread and potatoes.
Each evening baskets
of broken dinner hit the disposal unit.

Four children, product of two marriages,
two wives, countless slighter relations
and friends all come to the table

bringing new wines discovered on holiday,
fresh thirtyish faces, the chopped
Japanese dip of perfectly nourished hairstyles,
more children, more confident voices,
wave after wave consuming the table.

The writer's son

The father is a writer; the son
(almost incapable of speech)
explores him.

'Why did you take my language
my childhood
my body all sand?

why did you gather my movements
waves pouncing
eyes steering me till I crumbled?

We're riveted. I'm in the house
hung up with verbiage like nets.
A patchwork monster at the desk
bending the keys of your electric typewriter.

You're best at talking. I know
your hesitant, plain vowels.
Your boy's voice, blurred,
passed through my cot bars, stealing my baby magic.
You were the one they smiled at.'

Ollie and Charles at St Andrew's Park

Up at the park once more
the afternoon ends.
My sister and I huddle in quilted jackets.

A cigarette burn
crinkles the pushchair waterproofs,
the baby relaxes
sucking his hood's curled edges.

Still out of breath
from shoving and easing the wheels
on broken pavement we stay here.
Daffodils break in the wintry bushes

and Ollie and Charles in drab parkas
run, letting us wait by the swings.
Under eskimo hoods their hair springs
dun coloured, child-smelling.

They squat, and we speak quietly,
occasionally scanning the indigo patched
shadows with children melted against them.

Winter fairs

The winter fairs are all over.
The smells of coffee and naphtha
thin and are quite gone.

An orange tossed in the air
hung like a wonder
everyone would catch once,

the children's excitable cheeks
and woollen caps that they wore
tight, up to the ears,
are all quietened, disbudded;

now am I walking the streets
noting a bit of gold paper? –
a curl of peel suggesting the whole
aromatic globe in the air.

In a wood near Turku

The summer cabins are padlocked.
Their smell of sandshoes
evaporates over the lake water
leaving pine walls to shoulder the ice.

Resin seals them in hard splashes.
The woodman
knocks at their sapless branches.

He gets sweet puffballs
and chanterelles in his jacket,
strips off fungus like yellow leather,
thumbs it, then hacks the tree trunk.

Hazy and cold as summer dawn
the day goes on,

wood rustles on wood,
close, as the mist thins
like smoke around the top of the pine trees
and once more the saw whines.

Landscape from the Monet Exhibition at Cardiff

My train halts in the snowfilled station.
Gauges tick and then cease
on ice as the track settles
and iron-bound rolling stock creaks.

Two work-people
walk up alongside us,
wool-wadded, shifting their picks,

the sun, small as a rose,
buds there in the distance.
The gangs throw handfuls of salt like sowers
and light fires to keep the points moving.

Here are trees, made with two strokes.
A lady with a tray of white teacups
walks lifting steam from window to window.

I'd like to pull down the sash and stay
here in the blue where it's still work time.
The hills smell cold and are far away
at standstill, where lamps bloom.

Breakfast

Often when the bread tin is empty
and there's no more money for the fire
I think of you, and the breakfast you laid for me
– black bread and honey and beer.

I threw out a panful of wine yesterday –
the aluminium had turned sour –
I have two colours of bread to choose from,
I'd take the white if I were poor,

so indigence is distant as my hands
stiff in unheated washing water,
but you, with your generous gift of butter
and cheese with poppy seeds, all in one morning meal

have drawn the blinds up at the bedside window
and I can watch the ships' tall masts appear.

Index

(Titles and subtitles are in italics,
first lines in roman type.)

A barefoot girl hugs the wall   21
A Bit of Love   43
A candle for the ship's breakfast   203
A cow here in the June meadow   390
A draught like a bony finger   274
A dream of wool   333
A fat young man in BERBER'S ICE
   CREAM PARLOUR   314
A heap of cloud   99
A Loose Curl   40
A lorry-load of stuff   170
A May evening and a bright moon
   162
A meditation of the glasshouses   338
A mortgage on a pear tree   326
A pæony truss on Sussex place   337
A pear tree stands in its own maze
   326
A pretty shape   217
A safe light   414
A skater comes to this blue pond   382
A wash of stars covers the sky   161
A winter imagination   148
Adders   248
After a night jagged by guard-dogs and
   nightingales   297
After all they didn't taste of salt   159
After midday the great lazy   363
Afterword   269
Agapanthus above Porthmeor   93
Ahead of us, moving through time   381
Ahvenanmaa   240
Air layering   336
All the breaths of your life   55
All the squares of trampoline are taken
   227
All the things you are not yet   214
All through sour soil the gorse thrusts
   151
All you who are awake in the dark of
   the night   92
Almost island and jewel of all islands
   59
Always rain, September rain   68
An Irish miner in Staffordshire   350
And besides, we might play cards   20
And now we come to the unknown
   land   50

And this is where they met in secret
   55
And what a load of leaf   149
And when at last the voyage was over
   24
Annunciation off East Street   392
Approaches to winter   404
Are they blue or not blue?   39
As good as it gets   191
At Cabourg   329
At Cabourg II   295
At Ease   90
At Great Neck one Easter   391
At the Emporium   204
At the Spit   49
At three in the morning   353
Athletes   149

Babes in the Wood   261
Baby sleep   219
Barclays Bank, St Ives   100
Barnoon   136
Baron Hardup   296
Basement at Eighteen Folgate Street   99
Basketball player on Pentecost Monday
   221
Bathing at Balnacarry   258
Beautiful John Donne   103
Beautiful today the   142
Because she told a lie, he says   189
Beetroot Soup   255
Below Hungerford Bridge   156
Beneath the bulk of the block the bins
   89
Bewick's swans   381
Big barbershop man   304
Bildad   96
Blackberries after Michaelmas   152
Blue against blue; blue into deeper blue
   93
Bluebell Hollows   39
Boatman   79
Borrowed light   147
Bouncing boy   227
Boys on the Top Board   259
Breakfast   422
Breast to breast against the azaleas
   240

424

Breeze of ghosts   284
Bridal   154
Bride in the mud of the yard   154
Bristol Docks   186
Brown coal   301
But tell me, Elpenor   26
By chance I was alone in my bed the
  morning   234

Cajun   262
Candle poem   203
Candlemas   349
Christmas caves   274
Christmas roses   355
City lilacs   125
Clearing the mirror to see your face
  195
Cliffs of Fall   58
Clinic day   403
Close to the earth, creeping, lowly   44
Cloud   115
Code-breaking in the Garden of Eden
  321
Coiled peel goes soft on the deserted
  table   417
Cold pinches the hills around Florence
  384
Come Out Now   76
Convolvulus   129
Cool as sleep, the crates ring   403
Counting Backwards   19
Cowboys   156
Crossing the field   126
Cursing softly and letting the matches
  drop   374
Cutting open the lemons   159
Cyclamen, blood-red   174
Dancing man   293

Dark, present, scattering night   95
Dead gull on Porthmeor   143
Death, hold out your arms for me   70
Decoding a night's dreams   333
Dedication   60
Deep in busy lizzies and black iron
  243
Dense slabs of braided-up lupins   343
Depot   170

Dis   88
Diving girl   216
Do they wake careless and warm   288
'Doesn't it look peaceful?' someone said
  133
Dolphins whistling   145
Domestic poem   400
Don't count John among the dreams   128
Drink and the Devil   239
Driving along the motorway   138
Dropped yolks of shore-lamp quiver on
  tarmac   310
Dublin 1971   344
Dumb, his lips swathed   354

Everything changes to black and white
  144

Fallen angel   153
Father, / I remember when you left us
  261
February 12th 1994   53
Ferns on a hospital window   215
Festival of stone   42
First, the echo   213
First, the retreat of bees   173
Fishing beyond sunset   208
Five Versions from Catullus   59
Florence in permafrost   384
For all frozen things   328
For the length of time it takes a bruise
  to fade   127
For those who do not write poems
  132
For three years I've been wary of deep
  water   364
Fortune-teller on Church Road   193
Four cormorants, one swan   51
From behind the curtain an open
  window   215
Frostbite   220
'Fuck this staring paper and table   410

Getting into the car   137
Getting the Strap   247
Ghost at noon   227
Giraffes in Hull   167
Girl in the Blue Pool   52

425

Give me that red tub like a child's drawing   79

Glad of these times   138

Gorse   151

Greek beads   228

Greenham Common   409

Harbinger   91

Hare in the snow   208

'Has she gone then?' they asked   346

He is the one you can count on   204

He lived next door all his life   205

He must stir himself. No more hiding   43

He takes the temperature of his heart   100

He wears a silver bell   108

He's going on holiday to lonely   236

Hearing owls   160

Heimat   243

Her children look for her   56

Her fast asleep face turns from me   415

Here at my worktop, foil-wrapping a silver salmon   207

Here I am in the desert knowing nothing   244

Here is the bowl. Do I want it still   62

Here they are on the beach where the boy played   48

Here, where the old Industrial School was   37

Heron   308

Herring girl   282

Hold out your arms   70

Holiday to Lonely   236

Hornsea, 1952   41

How busy we are with the dead in their infancy   112

How cool the lovely bulb of your roundness   141

How hushed the sentence is this morning   196

How rangy they are, and lean, these leaves   206

How the sick body calms itself   315

Hungry Thames   224

I am the captainess of laundry   110

I can't say why so many coffin-makers   198

I don't need to go to the sun   29

I dreamed my love became a boat   157

I have a little sister, she has no breasts   54

I Have Been Thinking of You So Loudly   115

I have never known you easily   40

I Heard You Sing in the Dark   119

I hung up the sheets in moonlight   414

I imagine you sent back from Africa   356

I know that no one dare judge another's need   209

I know them by their shoes   99

I lay and heard voices   273

I love it when you look at me like this   155

I love these flowers that lie in the dust   129

I never stop listening to you sing   217

I Owned a Woman Once   80

I remember years ago, that we had Christmas roses   355

I see the boys at the breakwater   296

I should like to be buried in a summer forest   212

I was in the kingdom of pointed raspberries   225

I was up and watching   102

I'd climbed the crab-apple in the wind   310

I've approached him since childhood   359

Ice coming   173

If I wanted totems, in place of the poles   264

If I were the moon   57

If no revolution come   412

If only   192

If you had said the words 'to the forest'   316

If you lie down at the Spit on this warm   49

If you were to reach up your hand   132

In a back garden I'm painting   397

In a wood near Turku   420
In Berber's Ice Cream Parlour   314
In crack-haunted alleys, overhangs   125
In deep water   364
In memoriam Cyril Smith 1913-1945   359
In Praise of the Piano   22
In Rodmell Garden   396
In Secret   55
In such meadows the days pass   34
In the chemist's at night-time   406
In the corded hollows of the wood   313
In the Desert Knowing Nothing   244
In the dusk of a forest chapel   358
In the goods yard the tracks are unmarked   389
In the tea house   383
In the tents   377
In the weightlessness of time and our passage within it   367
In the white sheets I gave you   249
'Indeed we are all made from the dust of stars'   140
Inside out   199
Inside the Wave   24
Is it Lethe or is it dock water?   109
'It is finished,' said Christ   175
It is the same electrical impulse as ever   78
It is your impulse I remember   155
It starts with breaking into the wood   278
It was not always a dry well   305
It was the green lorry with its greasy curtain   170
It was too hot, that was the argument   336
It was you I heard, your tiger pad on the stairs   197
It wears a smell of earth, not air   118
It's evening on the river   308
It's not the four-wheeled drive crawler   331
It's past nine and breakfast is over   396
Its big red body ungulps   255

Jacketless, buckled, pressed from the voyage   64

Jacob's drum   168

La Recouvrance   120
Lady Macduff and the primroses   365
Lambkin   344
Landscape from the Monet Exhibition at Cardiff   421
Later my stepson will uncover a five-inch live shell   329
Lazarus   354
Lead me with your cold, sure hand   233
Leave the door open   30
Lemon and stars   159
Lemon sole   273
Lemon tree in November   95
Let us think that we are pilgrims   349
Lethe   109
Life and death are in the hands of God she said   56
Litany   127
Little Ellie and the timeshare salesman   226
Little papoose   57
Long long I have looked for you   277
Longman English Series   82
Lutherans   317

Malta   348
Mary Shelley   367
May voyage   162
Melancholy at one A.M.   158
Mimosa   45
Missile launcher passing at night   386
Mr Lear has left a ring in his room   192
Mr Lear's ring   192
Music plays gently   229
My daughter as Penelope   35
My life's stem was cut   31
My mind aches where I cannot touch it   158
My nephews with almond faces   408
My people   67
My sad descendants   373
My slim volume, polished almost to nothing   60
My train halts in the snowfilled station   423

Narcissi   144
Nature came to us abhorring sharp
    edges   115
Near Dawlish   415
Nearly May Day   297
Need   209
New crops   334
Newgate   89
Next door   204
Nightfall in the IKEA Kitchen   46
No matter how wide the snowfield   94
No one else remembers that room   53
No, not a demonstration   140
No, they won't gather their white skirts
    137
Not going to the forest   316
Now I write off a winter of growth
    404
Now the snowdrop, the wood-anemone,
    the crocus   365
Now winter comes and I am half-asleep
    224

O engines   334
O that old cinema of memory   169
O wintry ones, my sad descendants   373
Odysseus   132
Odysseus to Elpenor   26
Of course they're dead, or this is a film
    238
Off the West Pier   310
Off-script   140
'Often they go just before dawn'   161
Often when the bread tin is empty   424
Old Jeffery begins his night music   339
Old men with sticks and courteous
    greeting   100
Old warriors and women   185
Ollie and Charles at St Andrew's Park
    419
On circuit from Heptonstall Chapel   341
On drinking lime juice in September   315
On growing a black tulip   225
On his skin the stink   239
On looking through the handle of a cup
    63
On not writing certain poems   291
On smooth buttercup fields   350

On the other side of the sky's dark
    room   129
On the same posts each evening   111
On the white path at noon when the
    sun   227
One A.M.   158
One more for the beautiful table   343
One year he painted his front door
    yellow   205
One yellow chicken   309
Ophelia   157
Our day off, agreed by the wind   377
Our family, swimming again   306
Out of the Blue   165

Patrick at four years old on Bonfire Night
    374
Patrick, I cannot write   401
Patrick I   401
Patrick II   402
Pedalo   251
Permafrost   328
Pharaoh's daughter   399
Pianist, 103,   101
Picture Messages   108
Pictures of a Chinese nursery   398
*Piers Plowman: The Crucifixion &
    Harrowing of Hell*   175
Pilgrims   349
Plane tree outside Ward 78   28
Playing Her Pieces   100
Ploughing the roughlands   331
Plume   132
Pneumonia   149
Poem for December 28   408
Poem for hidden women   410
Poem in a Hotel   237
*Poem on the Obliteration of 100,000 Iraqi
    Soldiers*   245
Porpoise washed up on the beach   363
Preaching at Gwennap   340
Pressed in the soil's black web, nursed
    by the rough   91
Prince Felipe Prospero (1657-1661)   108
Privacy of rain   292

Rain. A plump splash   292
Rapunzel   379

Re-opening the old mines 23
Refrigerator days 222
Restless, the pæony truss tosses about 327
Rim 62
Rinsing 313
Rubbing Down the Horse 241
Russian doll 283

Safe period 303
Sailing to Cuba 310
St Paul's 407
Say we're in a compartment at night 190
Scan at 8 weeks 250
Seal run 323
Second marriages 416
See this 'un here, this little bone needle 282
See, you have fallen asleep in spite of me 307
September Rain 68
Seven years old last birthday 35
Shadows of my mother against a wall 335
She comes close to perfection 191
She kept Uncle Will's telegram 378
She swam to me smiling, her teeth 251
She's next to nowhere, feeling no cold 216
Ships on brown water 186
Shutting the Gate 21
Sirmio 59
Sisters leaving before the dance 289
Skips 264
Skulking 99
Sleeveless 194
Small, polished shield-bearer 91
Small, silvery, slipping 228
Smoke 185
Snow Queen 277
Snowdrops, Mary's tapers 349
Snug as a devil's toenail embedded 199
So, how decisive a house is 400
Some swear by vinegar and some by newspaper 118

Sometimes in the rough garden of city spaces 211
Sometimes, but rarely, the ancestors 134
Spanish Irish 155
Sparrow 61
Speak to me in the only language 165
Spring of turf and thrift, tangle of fleece, sheep-shit 58
Step by step, holding the thread 121
Still as the water is 113
Still life with ironing 155
Subtraction 66
Such a connoisseur of borrowed light! 147
Surely it's not too much to ask 148
Sweet pepper 307
Sylvette Scrubbing 260

Taken in Shadows 103
Tall ship hanging out at the horizon 284
Tea at Brandt's 229
Ten Books 64
Terra Incognita 50
That dream when we were young 94
That lake lies along the shore 293
That morning when the potato tops rusted 246
That old cinema of memory 169
That violet-haired lady 275
That's better, he says, he says 344
The air-blue gown 371
The apple fall 397
The argument 336
The bald glasshouses stretch here for miles 338
The Bare Leg 32
The bathers, where are they? 295
The Bike Lane 238
The blessing 200
The blue garden 133
The boy in the boat, the tip of the pole 208
The bride's nights in a strange village 353
The butcher's daughter 279
The Captainess of Laundry 110

The chink of hammers is a song   42
The coffin-makers   198
The conception   249
The cuckoo game   278
The damson   395
The dark fabric of night not torn   160
The dark, present, scattering night   96
The Day's Umbrellas   111
The Deciphering   112
The deserted table   417
The Diving Reflex   256
The dream-life of priests   287
The dry glasshouse is almost empty
   337
The dry well   305
The Duration   48
The father is a writer; the son   418
The Filament   121
The footfall   197
The form   195
The Gift   113
The grass looks different in another
   country   345
The greenfield ghost   281
The grey lilo   130
The halls are thronged, the grand
   staircase murmurous   200
The Halt   38
The hard-hearted husband   346
The haunting of Epworth   339
The horse landscape   375
The Hyacinths   91
The Inbox   78
The Kingdom of the Dead   116
The knight   358
The Lamplighter   37
The land pensions   332
The last day of the exhausted month   415
The Last Heartbeat   117
The long arm hangs flat to his lap   342
The Malarkey   75
The man on the roof   166
The man who gave little Ellie his
   forever   226
The mare with her short legs heavily
   mud-caked   341
The marshalling yard   389

The midwife whose omniscient hands
   403
The night chemist   406
The Night Workers   92
The obvious story, my darling   88
The Old Mastery   117
The other babies were more bitter than
   you   402
The other side of the sky's dark room
   129
The Our Father, the moment of fear
   247
The Overcoat   118
The panting of buses through caves of
   memory   170
The parachute packers   361
The peach house   337
The Place of Ordinary Souls   34
The plum tree   370
The point of not returning   194
The Polish husband   393
The potatoes come out of the earth
   bright   323
The Queue's Essentially   110
The rain was falling down in slow
   pulses   336
The rain's coming in   190
The room creaked like a pair of lungs
   301
The rowan   135
The scattering   213
The schooner *La Recouvrance* is almost
   at the horizon now   120
The sea skater   382
The sea's a featureless blaze   348
The sentence   196
The shaft   29
The Silent Man in Waterstones   265
The slowly moving river in summer
   399
The Snowfield   94
The soft fields part in hedges, each
   386
The spill   188
The stars come so close   159
The summer cabins are padlocked   422
The surgeon husband   207

430

The swans go up with slow wing-beats 51

The Tarn 113

The thing about a saddle is that second 241

The Torn Ship 102

The traffic halted 393

The tree outside the window 28

The Underworld 20

The Wardrobe Mistress 266

The wasp 224

The white receiver 250

The window swings and squeaks in the sun 392

The winter fairs are all over 420

The wood-pigeon rolls soft notes off its breast 335

The writer's son 418

The Yellow Sky 246

Then I think how the train 263

There he stands, blind on slivovitz 194

There is a gargoyle look when the mouth caves 55

There we sat in the clattering dark 32

There's a stone set in the car-park wall 172

These blackberries belong to the devil 152

These second marriages arching within 416

Thetis 376

They are building houses 140

They are hiding away in the desert 245

They are the sun's fingerprints on grey pebbles 131

They fly / straight-necked and barely white 276

They make him a plaster saint of poetry 83

They rode the ridge those five minutes 156

This evening clouds darken the street quickly 407

This is Jacob's drum 168

This is the wardrobe mistress, touching 266

This is what I want 262

This path is silky with dust 248

Those shady girls 287

Those words like oil, loose in the world 188

Three Ways of Recovering a Body 234

Three workmen with blue pails 300

Through Babel of Nations 59

Tiger lookout 222

Tiger Moth caterpillar 223

Time by Accurist 264

To Betty, swimming 313

To cross the field on a sunset of spider-webs 126

To my nine-year-old self 152

To Virgil 233

Today in a horse landscape 375

Today is barred with darkness of winter 409

Tonight I'm eating the past 371

Tonight there's a crowd in my head 214

Tulip 141

Two miles or so beyond 258

Two of us on the tired pavement 193

Two spines curve in 223

Uncle Will's telegram 378

Under the leaves 206

Undone 59

Untroubled, the anaesthetist 19

Up at the park once more 419

US 1st Division Airborne Ranger at rest in Honduras 342

Viking cat in the dark 218

Violets 134

Virgin with Two Cardigans 172

Visible and Invisible 94

Waist-deep in snow and wading 153

Waiting. I'm here waiting 237

Walking at all angles 167

Wall is the book 150

Washed silk jacket by Mesa 264

We are men, not beasts 230

We are the grown-ups, they the children 136

We stop somewhere on the plain   38
We're strung out on the plain's upthrust   312
Weaning   403
Weary and longing to go home   117
What I get I bring home to you   325
What shall I do for my sister in the day she shall be spoken for?   54
What Will You Say   114
What you have done to me has undone me   59
When I held you up to my cheek you were cold   283
When I should be working   82
When I was four at the feet   90
When my grandmother died my father eulogised her   166
When you grow tired of the flame   220
When You've Got   268
Where have you been, my little daughter   279
Where have you gone   395
Where the great ship sank I am   256
Whichever way I turned on the radio   317
Whooper swans   276
Why did you tell them to be quiet   75
Why is the mimosa here   45
Wild strawberries   325
Window Cleaners at Ladysmith Road   118
Winter 1955   312

Winter Balcony with Dunnocks   44
Winter bonfire   158
Winter fairs   420
With his hands he teaches wind to move   221
With short, harsh breaths   196
Without remission   189
Writ in Water   83

Years back and full of echoes   52
Yellow butterflies   131
Yes, but were we happy then?   41
Yes, we believed that the oceans were endless   145
Yesterday my stepson came home with school photographs   398
You always thought that you'd die mid-stride   66
You came back to life in its sweetness   242
You could use his wing as a fan   143
You must forgive me. Don't look so surprised   152
You never wanted the taste   113
You put your hand over mine and whispered   291
You're breast-up in the bubbling spaces you make for yourself   313
Your dry voice from the centre of the bed   303

Zelda   391